A Sense of Entry

A SENSE OF ENTRY

DESIGNING THE WELCOMING SCHOOL

Alan Ford and Paul Hutton
Text by Jennifer Seward

images
Publishing

Published in Australia in 2007 by
The Images Publishing Group Pty Ltd
ABN 89 059 734 431
6 Bastow Place, Mulgrave, Victoria 3170, Australia
Tel: +61 3 9561 5544 Fax: +61 3 9561 4860
books@imagespublishing.com
www.imagespublishing.com

Copyright © The Images Publishing Group Pty Ltd 2007
The Images Publishing Group Reference Number: 710

National Library of Australia Cataloguing-in-Publication entry:

Ford, Alan B.
A sense of entry: designing the welcoming school.

ISBN 978 186470 238 5

1. Entrance halls – United States – Designs and plans.
2. School buildings – United States – Designs and plans.
3. Architecture – United States. 4. Architectural firms –
United States. I. Hutton, Paul C. II. Seward, Jennifer.
III. Hutton Ford Architects. IV. Title.

727.0973

Edited by Melina Deliyannis

Designed by The Graphic Image Studio Pty Ltd, Mulgrave, Australia
www.tgis.com.au

Digital production by Splitting Image Colour Studio Pty Ltd, Australia
Printed by Sing Cheong Printing Co. Ltd., Hong Kong

IMAGES has included on its website a page for special notices in relation to this
and our other publications. Please visit www.imagespublishing.com

Photography: Ed LaCasse (pages 2–3)

C O N T E N T S

The meaning of entrance

The projects in this book are selected from our firm's work over the last 16 years. When designing schools we did not necessarily set out to feature the entrances or the movement systems. But it is now clear that our approach resulted in these features playing a key role in the architecture. The emphasis on entrances and movement systems is part of an overall strategy for high-performance school design that also includes proper daylighting, sustainability, and building designs that teach.

Our primary goal in designing schools is to create places that enhance the learning experience. In addition, we seek design solutions that are welcoming, solve programmatic and functional requirements, are environmentally responsible, and very importantly, acknowledge the significant role that the school facility plays in the lives of children and teachers. The building must also contribute to its place within the community. The entrance and movement architecture presented here is a natural outcome of all of these objectives.

The functions accommodated within the school have grown increasingly complex from the days of the one-room schoolhouse. Today a typical school incorporates facilities for dining, athletics, art, music, theater, administrative activities, libraries, science, and of course, traditional classroom activities. Often, the school's facilities are utilized after hours by the community for meetings and athletic activities. The mechanical, electrical, and data systems that support these activities have also become very complex. All of these requirements ultimately inform the design of the architecture.

Given the complexity of functions and the scale of a typical school today, we have found it is important to design the movement system in an intuitive, straightforward manner. The size of these schools dictates that one spends a lot of time moving within and around the school. Therefore, the awareness of movement has become a significant part of the daily experience in navigating the school environment. Making this experience as stress-free and enriching as possible is what *Designing the Welcoming School* is all about.

A brief history of architectural entrances

Architectural history shows that entrances have long been treated as important elements of design. Their significance is present in the earliest surviving buildings and is consistent across a wide variety of cultures and traditions. Modern architecture, or more precisely the International Style, is the notable exception. Even in its important buildings, entrances were not designed as welcoming events. Post-Modernism restored the prominence of entrances and even overstated them. We are now in a period of architecture that includes many different approaches to the entrance, from minimal to grand. Below are some notable buildings that we have found instructive in our search to develop the welcoming entrance.

INTRODUCTION

Temple of Hatshepsut, Luxor, Egypt, circa 1460 BCE

Ancient Egyptian architecture typically utilizes symmetry and grand scale with powerful effect. It is interesting to note that the center opening of the highest level is slightly wider than the twelve openings on either side. This subtle clue reinforces the location of the ceremonial entrance.

Parthenon, Athens, Greece, Iktinos and Kallikrates, 438 BCE

Placed atop the Acropolis, at the culmination of the Panathenaic Procession, the temple was considered in its time, and still today, the apogee of Greek architecture. The entrance is implied only by its central location under the peak of the pediment. In fact, any of the seven front openings created by the eight columns could function as entrance points. The Parthenon, along with many other classical structures, established the precedent in Western architecture that the entrance should occur at the center of the building, or at the center of a portion of a building. This may seem obvious, but is far from the case. Structural logic would place a column at the center to support the weight of the pediment and roof. The desire of the Greeks to place man at the center, and to measure all things relative to him, resulted in this approach.

Villa Poiana at Poiana Maggiorie, Vicenza, Italy, Andrea Palladio, 1548–49

Many forms utilized by Palladio became popular and have been used repeatedly throughout architectural history. These include the "Palladian motif" of a central arch flanked by lower rectangles as found at the Villa Poiana entrance. Each of Palladio's entrances was unique and in scale with the entire façade.

Gate, Kyoto, Japan, circa 15th century

The free-standing, post and beam form has a primary place in Japanese architecture. Rich in symbolism, the traditional Tori is a means of marking the entrance into a sacred place. Passing through it signifies an act of sanctification and purification. As utilized here, on a pathway in Kyoto, the use of repetitive but slightly varying post and beam elements, arranged on a straight axial path, creates a wonderful sense of procession.

top, left to right: Temple of Hatshepsut, Luxor, Egypt; Parthenon, Athens, Greece; Villa Poiana at Poiana Maggiorie, Vicenza, Italy; Gate, Kyoto, Japan
photography: *Sanjat Kanjilal; Alan Ford; Alan Ford; Stan Owocki*

Taj Mahal, India, 1643

The Taj Mahal is best known for its perfect symmetry, graceful proportions, and luxurious materials. The small entrance doors are framed within an arched opening of monumental scale. Once one finally reaches the doors, the richness and intricacy of the surface pattern leave one inspired, and set the tone for the interior architecture.

Pavilion IX at the Lawn, University of Virginia, Charlottesville, VA, USA, Thomas Jefferson, 1824

Of the ten pavilions originally used for faculty residences and classrooms that line Jefferson's Academical Village, this one is the most diminutive in scale. The other pavilions are examples of different classical orders and some are modeled on specific structures of antiquity. Pavilion IX is unique as it employs a curve in both plan and section, embracing the person entering. Standing at the center of the top step it is possible to extend one's arms and just touch both side walls. The recessed quarter sphere, painted a brilliant white, brings light deeper into the space and ultimately into the room behind.

One Room Schoolhouse, Douglas County, CO, USA, 1874

The One Room Schoolhouse, typical of early America and common across the Great Plains, became an enduring emblem of education and opportunity. There, any student able to make the trip, could learn and advance. The entrance was simple yet unmistakable with a covered doorway and vestibule.

Parque Guell, Barcelona, Spain, Antonio Gaudí, 1889

Gaudí brought a singular vision to his architecture. Based on the study of nature, it was a precursor to the Art Nouveau movement. His entrances are a natural outgrowth of the forms of the buildings themselves. The entrance to Parque Guell clearly marks a transition from one zone to another. While the mundane city resides outside, a land of fantastic forms and colors is found inside.

Porte Dauphine, Métro Station Entrance, Paris, France, Hector Guimard, 1899

Guimard is perhaps best known for his series of subway station entrances. Using Art Nouveau forms, his entrances have a sense of lightness and openness that contrasts starkly with the underground world beyond.

Helsinki Train Station, Helsinki, Finland, Eliel Saarinen, 1914

Saarinen's Helsinki train station is a fine example of late Classical architecture adapted to a new use. The station is concerned with movement at a previously unprecedented scale and speed. This is not just the entrance to a single building, but to a newly expanded world.

East High School, Denver, CO, USA, George Williamson, 1925

Of the four classically designed high schools in Denver, built within a few years of each other, East High is the finest example. This building clearly informs the city that what happens inside is important and should be valued.

Seagram Office Building, New York City, NY, USA, Mies van der Rohe with Philip Johnson, 1958

Considered the pinnacle of International Style design principles applied to the office structure, the Seagram has an understated but surprisingly effective entrance. The elevated, stone entry plaza, framed by symmetrical water features, presents an almost classical, formal entry experience. All of the senses are engaged, from the rhythm of the large-scale plaza pavers, to the sound and smell of the water jets that frame the path and buffer people as they make the transition from the automobile intensity of Park Avenue to the transparent business-like travertine lobby inside. The luminous quality of the regularly oiled bronze façade with the elegantly detailed, projected entry canopy, complete the very rich kinetic experience.

TWA Flight Center, New York City, NY, USA, Eero Saarinen, 1962

The best-known building example of Saarinen's Expressionist architecture is the TWA Flight Center. It consciously evokes the shape of a bird in flight, with the main entrance under the "tail" of the structure.

Yale Center for British Art, New Haven, CT, USA, Louis Kahn, 1972

Although Louis Kahn's buildings have more meaning than most masters of Modernism, his entrances are

top, left to right: Taj Mahal, India; Pavilion IX at the Lawn, University of Virginia, Charlottesville, VA, USA; One Room Schoolhouse, Douglas County, CO, USA; Parque Guell, Barcelona, Spain; Porte Dauphine, Métro Station Entrance, Paris, France | *photography:* Kerrie Kannberg; Paul Hutton; Paul Hutton; Alan Ford; Alan Ford
bottom, left to right: Helsinki Train Station, Helsinki, Finland; East High School, Denver, CO, USA; Seagram Office Building, New York City, NY, USA; TWA Flight Center, New York City, NY, USA; Yale Center for British Art, New Haven, CT, USA | *photography:* Alan Ford; Alan Ford; Howei Chan; Alan Ford; Shawn Szirbik

unfailingly minimal. The entrance to his Yale Center for British Art is little more than a dark void in the exterior wall. There is no way that visitors entering the building for the first time would imagine the wonderful interior spaces within.

Portland Public Service Building, Portland, OR, USA, Michael Graves, 1982

Michael Graves' Portland building was among the first examples of Post-Modernism at a large scale, and its entrance did not disappoint. Not only was it large in scale and prominently placed, it was further marked by a significant entry sculpture commissioned for the project.

AT&T Building, New York City, NY, USA, John Burgee Architects with Philip Johnson, 1984

The Philip Johnson-designed AT&T building was a breakout for Post-Modernism, and was pictured on the cover of *Time* magazine even before it was built. Although best known for its "Chippendale" top, its entrance was a soaring palladian-influenced archway in cut granite and glass. The vertically proportioned entrance lobby is marked by the iconic "Genius of

Electricity" sculpture by the artist Evelyn Beatrice. Philip Johnson understood full well the importance of procession in architecture and used it effectively here, creating a series of structurally layered outdoor rooms for the pedestrian to pass through prior to entering the building. Appropriately scaled for Manhattan, the entrance was a truly monumental gesture at a time when most office building entrances were barely noticeable.

Chiat/Day Building, Venice, CA, USA, Frank Gehry with Oldenburg and van Bruggen, 1985

Frank Gehry collaborated with artists known for creating oversized versions of everyday objects for this entrance to a parking garage and office building. The whimsical entrance accommodates both vehicles and pedestrians, and includes usable spaces within.

Louvre Museum, Paris, France, I.M. Pei, 1989

In reorganizing the visitor experience at the Louvre, I.M. Pei created an entirely new entrance for the historic complex. He superimposed a simplified and abstract pyramid form to contrast and also complement the Classical architecture all around. By creating a single point of entry and restructuring the internal circulation system there was now clarity to the

movement experience at the Louvre. The result was a significant increase in attendance to the museum.

Walt Disney Concert Hall, Los Angeles, CA, USA, Frank Gehry, 2003

Frank Gehry has invented his own set of architectural forms, which he has used masterfully. Although he avoids traditional entrance cues such as symmetrical or hierarchical forms, there is no doubt where the entrance is. It is found in the pronounced void of this undulating but solid surface. A grand set of steps leads visitors directly to the entrance, where the doors seem understated for a building of such prominence. The complex sculptural exterior forms continue through to the interior, but there is added richness through new materials and colors.

Elati Rail Maintenance Facility, Denver, CO, USA, RNL, 2004

The most recent trend to appear in entrance design is the greatly extended, often cantilevered, canopy. It shows up on all types of buildings, including libraries, museums, schools, and office buildings. It provides some protection from the elements and is an unmistakable beacon of entry. The distinctive, slightly inverted arc of the Elati entrance reaches out to greet visitors. While the upper canopy marks the entry point on the façade, the architect, by incorporating a double canopy, brought a very human scale to the entry experience.

Themes in our entrances

Although we approach every project as unique, there are consistent themes throughout our work. Our designs all include some portion of these four elements: Identity, Wayfinding, Influence of streets and Procession.

Identity

Perhaps the most important role of our entrance design is to tell the building's story along with the stories of its client, occupants, and community. As we begin a project we search for clues such as the architectural history of the neighborhood, cultural traditions in the community, favorite landmarks in the region, or interests of the occupants. From these clues we design a unique entrance form suited only to that particular project in that time and place.

Wayfinding

Some buildings depend on signage or other graphics to assist occupants and visitors in finding their way through a building. While some graphics are necessary, we believe the design of the building should be so intuitive that users understand where the main entrance is. They should also be able to navigate the interior of the building with minimal assistance. In designing buildings, we strive for clarity in the circulation system. We also build amenities into our circulation spaces so that they can be used for instruction.

Influence of streets

Our buildings vary in location from urban to rural. All of them are accessed from local streets and relate to these streets in a variety of ways. In the city, we may bring the building close to the street to create a wall. In the country, we may focus more on the relationship of one building to another. Occasionally the street orientation may influence the orientation of the building itself.

Procession

Although there is clearly a singular location that constitutes an "entry" in every building, we tend to think of the issue as more extended. We create layers of entrance both outside and inside the building. From the time one enters the site one is passing through these different layers. Although the main entrance is located at the transition from exterior to interior, there are also additional entrances within our buildings. These may be from a corridor into a special space such as a library, or from one zone of the building to another. We take care to provide architectural indications at these internal transitions, just as we take care in designing the main entrance. As a result, the building is experienced as a sequence of events as the occupant or visitor passes through successive entrances. Christopher Alexander in his well-known book, *A Pattern Language*, delineated another series of layers one experiences when entering a place, transitioning from the public to the semi-public to semi-private to the private realms. Procession may also be defined by the sense of rhythm that is naturally created by repetitive architectural or structural elements as a person moves through space. This can be found in the form of loggias, or for that matter, any repetitious form that lines a path. All of these elements make up what is referred to as "procession."

Practical considerations

Although the four themes above are the primary concerns of our entrance designs, we are also influenced by practical considerations. These considerations are related both to climate and to the needs of modern education. The practical objectives of our entrances include:

- Keeping out inclement weather—snow, rain, wind, heat, and cold. A vestibule with two sets of doors is most helpful in achieving this objective, so nearly all of our entrances include a vestibule. The vestibule becomes a room in its own right, with its own character. It is both inside and outside.
- Orienting entrances to the south, east, or west. In Colorado, weather protection is so critical that we prefer to orient entrances to the south. This minimizes

above: *Procession as seen in an Italian loggia*
photography: *Alan Ford*

build-up of snow and ice on walking surfaces. If that is not possible we select either east, or west. Only rarely have we designed a north-facing entrance.

- Providing a covered place to put on or remove outerwear. Many students and visitors arrive at our buildings wearing protective clothing. The lobby space just inside the building is the best place for this basic activity.
- Provide a secure entrance and building. We have increasingly focused on designing entrances that protect the building from unwelcome intrusion. This is achieved by locking all but the main entrance doors to prevent access from the outside. Administrative personnel also aid in monitoring the building by being located with a clear and unobstructed view of the parking lot and approach walk.
- Removing dirt from occupants' feet. We have learned that a deep vestibule with appropriate floor covering is necessary to keep dirt out of buildings and maintain good indoor air quality.
- Providing a transition from exterior lighting to interior lighting. In Colorado, light levels inside are often 1/100th of outside light levels during the day. Our entrances provide a transition where the light level is mid-way between full sunlight and interior lighting. At night this relationship is reversed. Then, the entrance provides a light level mid-way between interior light and nighttime light. This design approach gives the eye time to adjust.
- Providing a place to sit. Often students arrive before the school opens or must wait after school closes for a ride home. For them, seating sheltered from sun and rain is a valued amenity. As a result, most of our entrances include seating.
- Providing a means to dispose of trash. Providing a place to dispose of trash keeps our entrances cleaner.

We have learned that if we do not provide a litter container, the owner most often will.

- Identifying the building name and sometimes address. Local building codes require building identification and street address. We strive to include these in an integrated and elegant fashion.
- Identifying the architect and others involved in construction. There is a natural curiosity about every building. Who designed it, who built it, and when? We strive to answer these questions with a permanent plaque inside every entrance.

Conclusion

Historic school buildings often included powerful and hierarchical forms that conveyed the importance of the facility and its purpose. They created memorable architecture that also provided identity for the community. In the United States, public schools built since the 1950s have typically been more about utilitarian accommodation, with little investment in the architectural form. As a result, school buildings increasingly began to resemble office buildings and even factories.

School construction budgets are often stretched very thin due to the sheer extent of unmet need that has built up over the years. These budgets are usually insufficient to achieve memorable architecture. A major rethinking of our commitment to school construction funding will be necessary if we are to consistently create schools that tell the world that education is one of our most important tasks.

Alan Ford and Paul Hutton

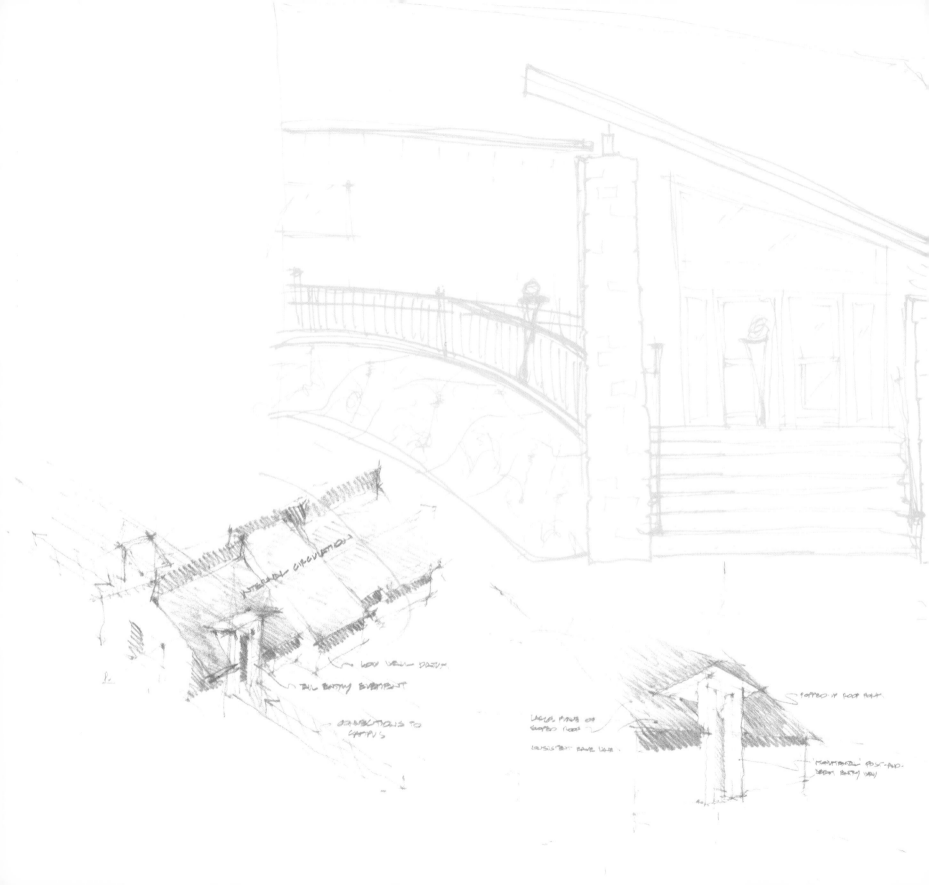

ALEXANDER DAWSON
SCHOOL

The 20-year-old gymnasium of the Alexander Dawson School was seriously lacking in architectural interest. In a dramatic rebirth, the pre-engineered metal building underwent a dynamic conversion to become the school's center for visual and performing arts.

The architects' challenge was to give the plain building a new identity, while leaving its metal shell intact. A 255-seat theater replaced the former basketball court, while a lobby, ticket booth, dance studio, dressing rooms, classrooms, workshops, and offices were added to the building.

Most significantly, the addition of a prominent new entrance marked by an elevated, glass-enclosed cube has given the Arts Center its distinctive character. Lifted high in the air, the cube serves as a beacon, announcing itself and drawing people in, especially at night. In a clever nod to the agricultural roots of the region, the cube appears to be a cab-on-a-farm combine. Others, recalling that the founder of the Dawson School was a pilot and aviation enthusiast who required students to take a class on aviation mechanics, prefer to see an airport control tower.

The lobby serves as a display gallery for student artwork where, once inside, visitors gaze up through the transparent cube to the sky beyond. The surprising contrast between the entry and the rest of the building provides a more contemporary feel, reflecting the artistic programs taking place inside.

ALEXANDER DAWSON
SCHOOL ARTS CENTER

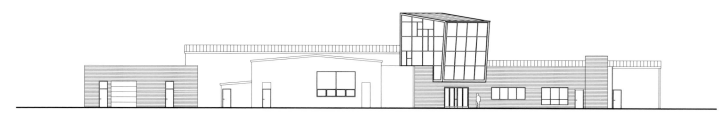

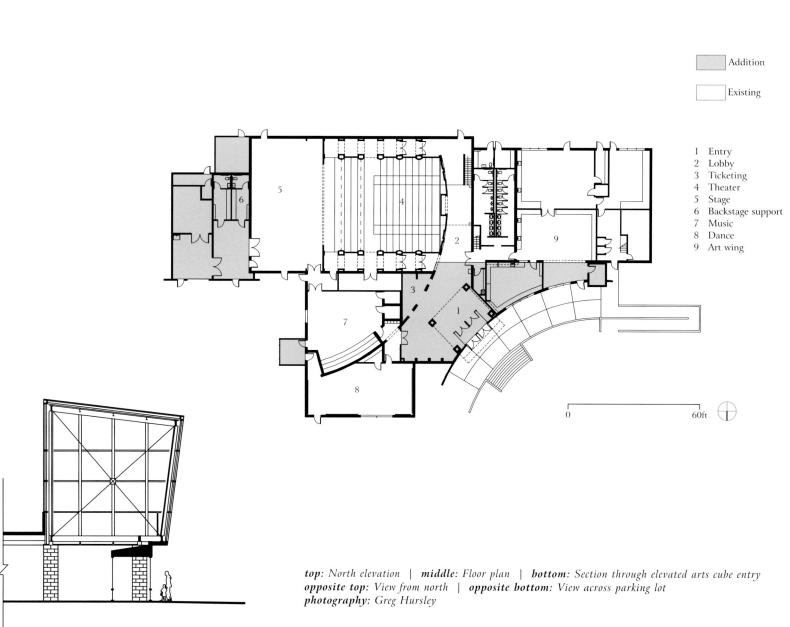

1 Entry
2 Lobby
3 Ticketing
4 Theater
5 Stage
6 Backstage support
7 Music
8 Dance
9 Art wing

Addition

Existing

0   60ft

top: North elevation | *middle:* Floor plan | *bottom:* Section through elevated arts cube entry
opposite top: View from north | *opposite bottom:* View across parking lot
photography: Greg Hursley

top: View from southwest | *middle:* West elevation
bottom: Section through main lobby
opposite: Evening view with Rocky Mountains in background

By far the bulkiest building on the Alexander Dawson Campus, the 30,000-square-foot gymnasium is located at the farthest corner of the grounds. The gymnasium is aligned with the lower school, tucked between playing fields and irrigation ponds.

The gymnasium was designed as two separate structures to keep the substantial complex from overwhelming the campus. The larger mass of the building—two adjoining gymnasiums—was pushed away from the campus, while the locker rooms, training rooms, and other support spaces were placed on the opposite side. A low-scaled shingle roof covers the campus side, reducing the apparent bulk of the gymnasium and blending it with the adjacent school buildings. Stone columns located at the main entrance visually link the gymnasium to the rest of the campus.

A skylight bridges the two opposing sides of the gymnasium and becomes an internal street, working powerfully to access all of the destinations inside. This low-budget building consistently elicits a "wow" response from first-time visitors. It provides the ideal home for the school's athletic programs and for sports enthusiasts.

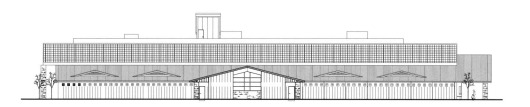

ALEXANDER DAWSON
SCHOOL GYMNASIUM

top: East elevation | *middle:* Section through gymnasium and corridor | *bottom left:* View from athletic fields
bottom right: Main corridor with weight room on left | *opposite top:* View from northeast with foothills in background
opposite bottom: Floor plan | *photography:* Greg Hursley

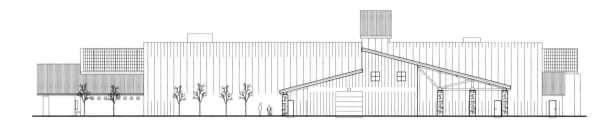

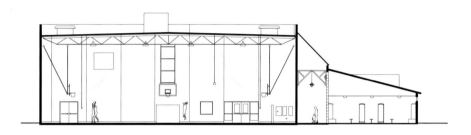

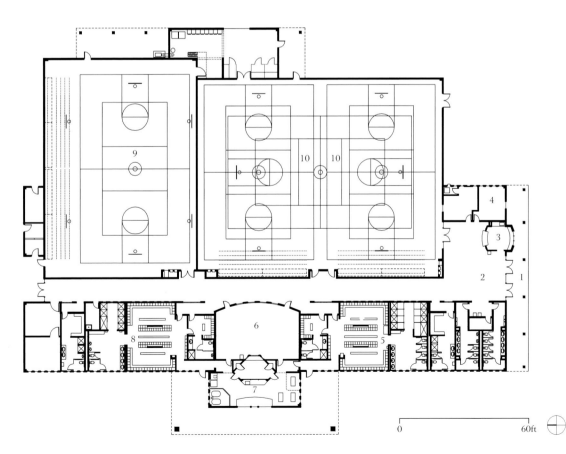

1 Covered entry
2 Lobby
3 Ticketing
4 Offices
5 Girls' locker room
6 Weight room
7 Training room
8 Boys' locker room
9 Auxiliary gymnasium
10 Main gymnasium

0   60ft

As Hutton Ford Architects' design approach continued to evolve on the Alexander Dawson campus, the school's vision was also growing. When an elementary school was added, it had to meet the needs of kindergarten through fourth grade. The building is located at the opposite end of campus from the middle school. The two function as bookends, each one providing a visual termination for the main campus walkway. The entrance forms are deliberately similar to reinforce this relationship.

Like the middle school, the lower school has two entrances. The front door welcomes pedestrians arriving from the campus, while the back door faces the parking lot and greets parents and visitors arriving by car or bus. Also like the middle school, a kiva sits at the center of the circulation network, encouraging intimate gatherings for story time, meetings or entertainment such as a puppet show.

A curved main interior street links the two entrances. The kindergarten playground anchors one end, while the exit on the other end leads students to the gym and an outdoor plaza. A defining aspect of the lower school is its strong relationship of inside to outside space. Students are visually connected to the outdoors from anywhere inside the school.

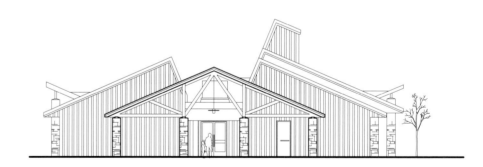

ALEXANDER DAWSON
LOWER SCHOOL

top left: *West entrance from campus axis* | ***top right:*** *View from northwest* | ***bottom:*** *South elevation* | ***opposite top:*** *Site plan*
opposite bottom: *Campus circulation diagram*

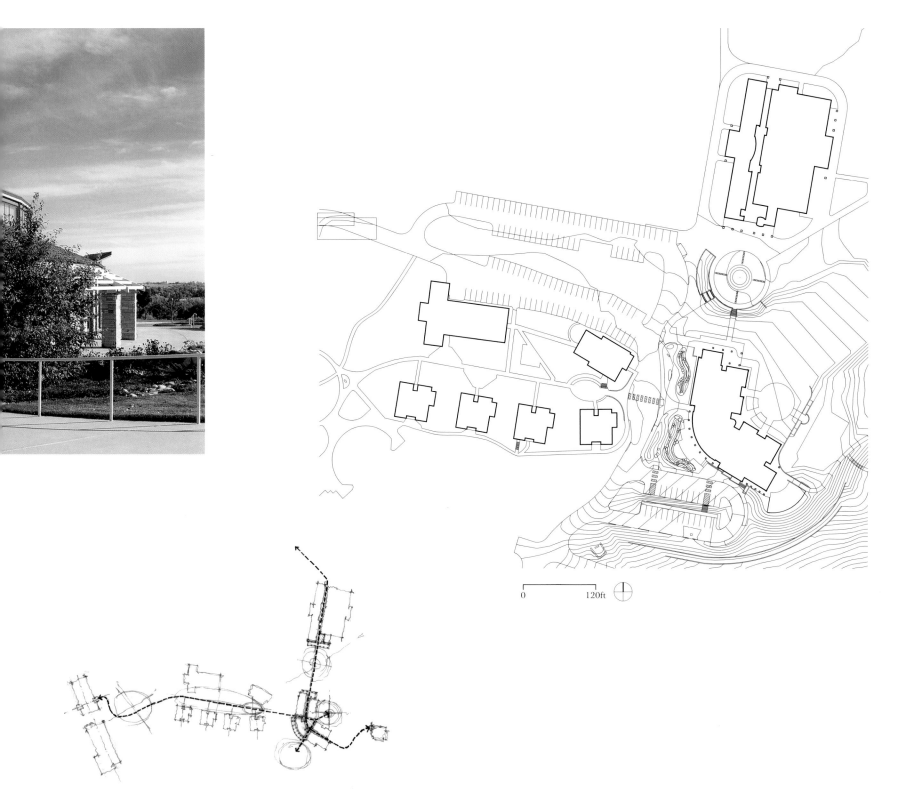

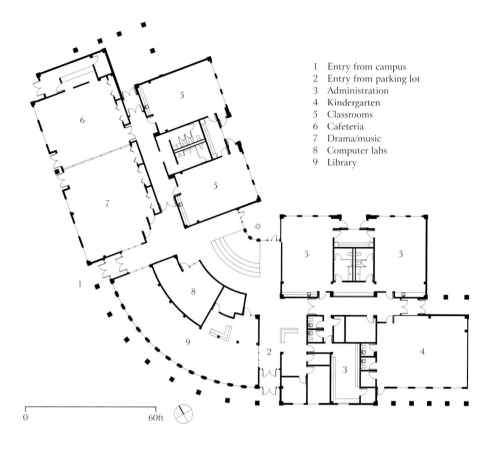

1   Entry from campus
2   Entry from parking lot
3   Administration
4   Kindergarten
5   Classrooms
6   Cafeteria
7   Drama/music
8   Computer labs
9   Library

0   60ft

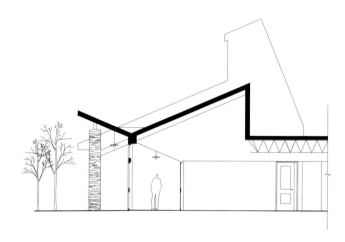

opposite top left: Floor plan | *opposite top right:* Section through main entrance | *opposite bottom left:* Typical daylit classroom
opposite bottom middle: Kindergarten classroom | *opposite bottom right:* Model showing hill in foreground | *above:* View of library with Xeriscape in foreground
photography: Greg Hursley

Hutton Ford Architects worked non-stop on the Dawson School for nearly 13 years. Its mission: to completely transform the jumble of seemingly unrelated buildings into a campus. The design team was challenged to work with the schools' existing architecture, where buff sandstone, wood shake roofs and wood siding made a person feel at home. Dawson Middle School—the first completely new building on the campus in 15 years—upholds this western theme, finely tuned to establish a stronger sense of place.

The school's front and back entrances were given equal importance. The front door faces the pedestrian side; the back door is located directly across from the front entrance, overlooking the vehicular side, or parking lot. The main lobby connects these distinctive entrances, strategically providing administrators a place to greet visitors as well as to monitor and control movement.

While not grandiose in size, the entrance is unmistakable and is appropriate in scale for the users of the building. The same form was used later at both the library and the lower school.

Panoramic views of the Rocky Mountains and surrounding campus are visible from anywhere inside the school. The basic classrooms, science lab, and computer lab all feature sloping ceilings and broad clerestory windows. It was important to the architects that students be able to find their way easily around the school. The design generates a perpendicular circulation system with two significant gathering spaces —or kivas—at the mid-point and terminus of the system. The kivas offer informal seating for activities, meetings, and more.

ALEXANDER DAWSON MIDDLE SCHOOL

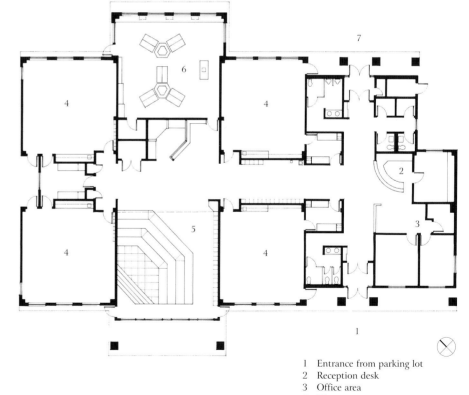

opposite: Entrance from campus | ***top:*** *View from parking lot* | ***bottom:*** *Floor plan*
photography: *Greg Hursley (page 32); Andrew Kramer (page 33)*

1 Entrance from parking lot
2 Reception desk
3 Office area
4 Classroom
5 Kiva
6 Science lab
7 Entrance from campus

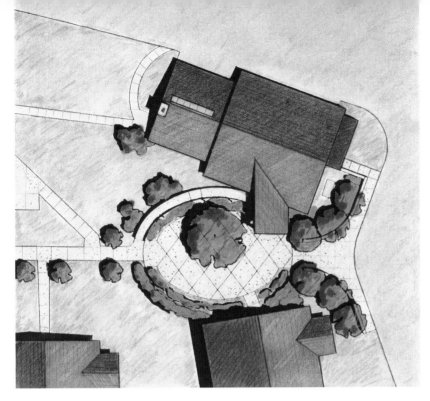

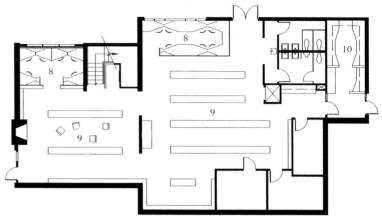

1 Entry
2 Reading lounge
3 Conference room
4 Office
5 Circulation desk
6 Look-up
7 Reference
8 Study carrels
9 Stacks
10 IT office

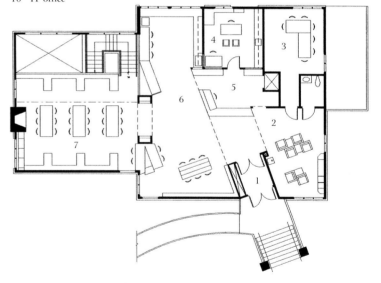

ALEXANDER DAWSON
SCHOOL LIBRARY

opposite top left: Site plan | *opposite top right:* Ground floor plan | *opposite bottom left:* Main entry
opposite bottom right: Entry level floor plan | *above:* Interior entry arch at reading room
photography: Paul Hutton (page 34); Andrew Kramer (page 35)

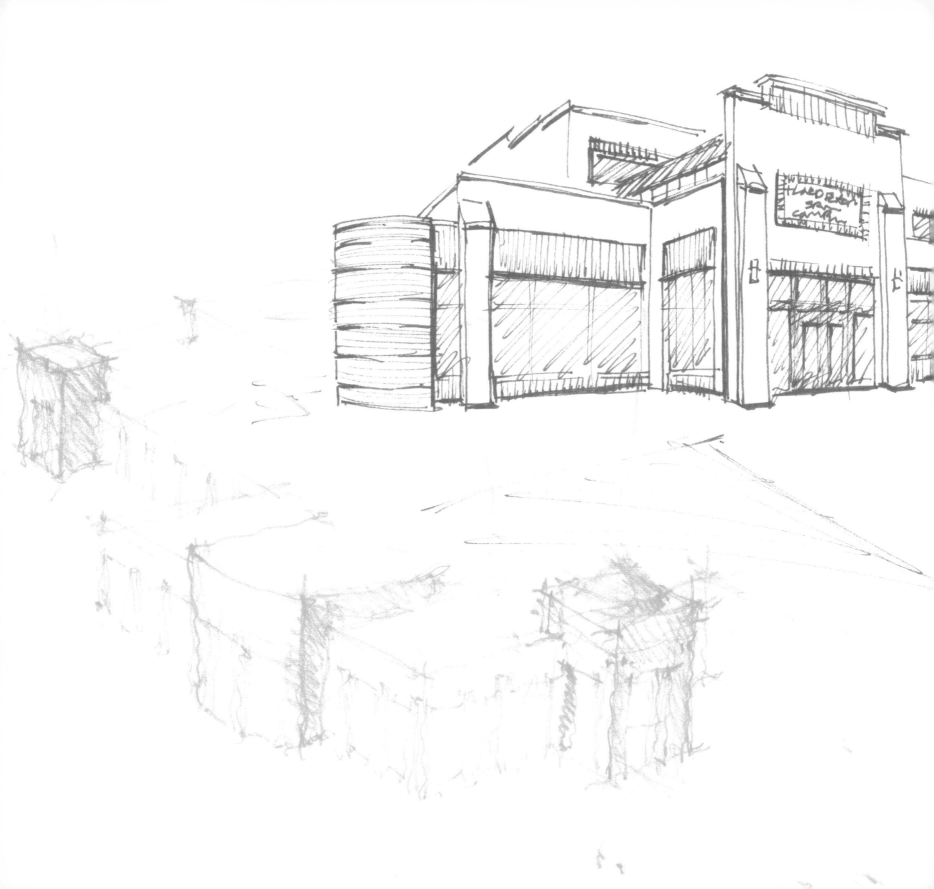

FORT LUPTON
EDUCATIONAL CAMPUS

ENTRY BRICK TO
MATCH EXISTING FIELD
BRICK

BRICK ACCENT
(MATCH ADDITION)

STL. CANOPY

ALIGN w/ EXIST.
ENTRY PLAZA

Each of the entrances for this large multiple-addition project on the Fort Lupton Campus took on a character consistent with the architecture of its respective building, ranging from 1930's to 1970's design styles. While buff and umber colored brick serve as the common link to unify the grounds, the historic forms of the original buildings also helped to define the new designs.

Fort Lupton Butler Elementary School

The architecture of the old middle school—a revered community landmark on the Fort Lupton educational campus—helped to inform the new design of Butler Elementary. Masonry piers, along with buff and umber-colored brick, serve as the common link that unifies the campus, seamlessly joining elementary, middle, and high schools with the administration building and pool. Once this neutral base was established, Butler Elementary's entry took on a cheerful quality, particularly fitting for young children.

The entrance is playful, offering a lighthearted first impression with its unexpected color, castle-like crenellations, and candy striping. Blue-glazed brick bands the school's exterior and a whimsical weather vane perches on the conical roof.

FORT LUPTON
EDUCATIONAL CAMPUS

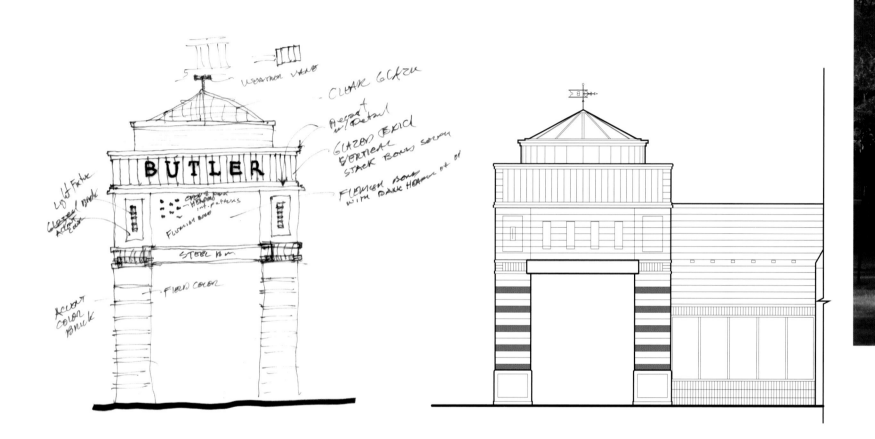

left: Design sketch | ***right:*** Front elevation | ***opposite left:*** Close-up of entrance tower | ***opposite top right:*** North elevation
opposite bottom right: View looking up to skylight

top: Skylight inside ellipse in front of library | *bottom:* Main reception desk
opposite: View from corridor into library

Floyd E. Acre Sports Complex

The sports complex includes a high school gymnasium and an elementary school gymnasium. The community also uses the complex after hours. The main entry was designed to align with the existing high school entrance and is adjacent to a large parking area. The sports complex entry extends toward the high school entry, creating a sunny outdoor courtyard where the two come together. Students are drawn to this spot, gathering for lunch or to study under the grid of honey locust trees.

Masonry piers, which are derived from the original 1930's campus building, define the entry. A barrel-vault roof provides a greater sense of space inside the gym entry, terminating the 300-foot main corridor and echoing both the gym roof shape and the apse feature at the end of the corridor.

Fort Lupton High School Entrance

The primary road from town to the educational campus passes by the middle school building before visually terminating on axis with the high school and a large circular drive. The drive serves as a bus drop-off for the high school and the elementary school. Because the high school was the largest building on campus and featured prominently from the main road, the architects felt it deserved a more dynamic entrance statement. The original main entrance consisted of a door in a long glass corridor with no vestibule. The new entrance comes in the form of a simple, but prominent, "floating wall" anchored by a glass vestibule. The design maintains the simple unadorned character of the main building's architecture.

top and middle: *Detail of main entrance*
bottom: *North elevation* | **opposite:** *View from high school*

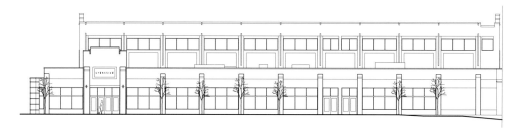

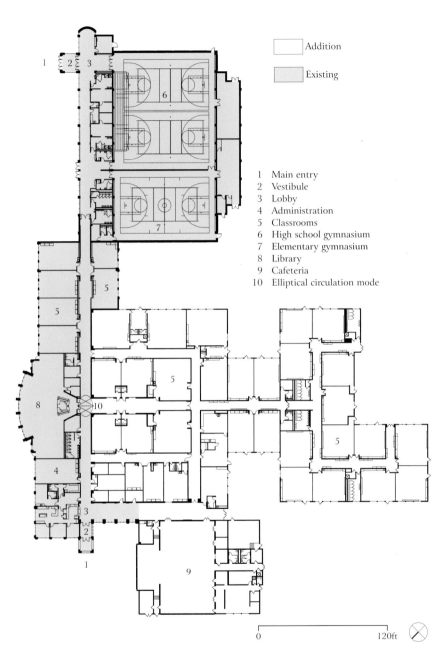

Addition

Existing

1 Main entry
2 Vestibule
3 Lobby
4 Administration
5 Classrooms
6 High school gymnasium
7 Elementary gymnasium
8 Library
9 Cafeteria
10 Elliptical circulation mode

0   120ft

left: View from parking lot | *above:* Floor plan

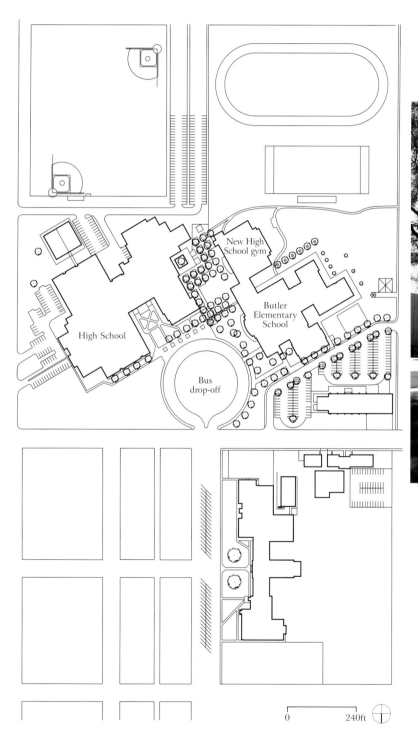

High School

New High School gym

Butler Elementary School

Bus drop-off

0   240ft

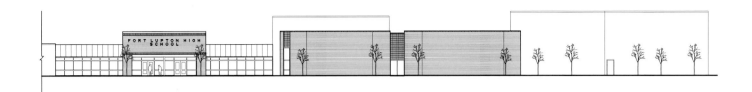

opposite left: Site plan | *opposite right:* Entrance from bus driveway | *top:* North elevation | *bottom:* Side view of new entrance
photography: Ed LaCasse (pages 38,39,41,42 top,43–46,48,49); Ron Johnson (page 42 bottom)

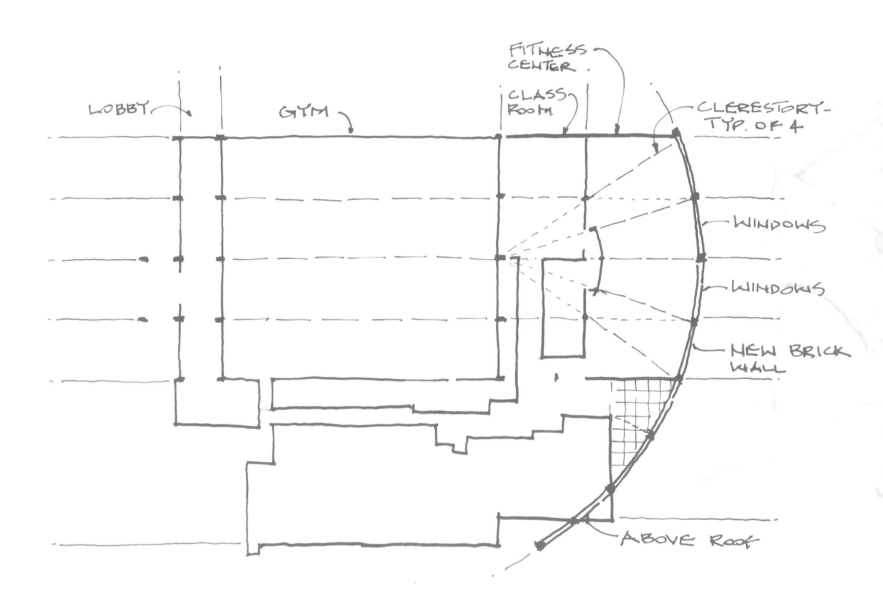

LOBBY

GYM

FITNESS CENTER.

CLASS ROOM

CLERESTORY- TYP. OF 4

WINDOWS

WINDOWS

NEW BRICK WALL

ABOVE ROOF

KENT DENVER SCHOOL

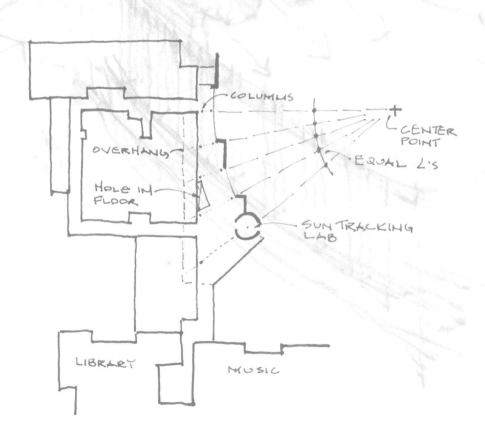

COLUMNS

CENTER
POINT

OVERHANG

EQUAL L's

HOLE IN
FLOOR

SUN TRACKING
LAB

LIBRARY

MUSIC

above: New fitness center entrance from fields | *opposite:* Curved wall extending over and beyond existing building

KENT DENVER FIELD HOUSE

*top: Curved wall and patio within | **bottom:** Fitness center entrance*
***right:** New fitness center with existing field house beyond*
***photography:** Matt Slater (page 52); Greg Hursley; (pages 53–55)*

The main entrance to the prestigious Kent Denver School was so understated that visitors were often unable to find it. Hutton Ford Architects strengthened the school's image through a new entry design, while also enlarging the student commons. A key element of the project entailed balancing the requirement for large assembly capacity with the students' need for a quiet refuge when studying.

The entrance merited a strong visual statement to anchor the expansive campus of six buildings and five parking lots. The new archway incorporates formal signage to effectively announce Kent's presence. While brick is used in a traditional and conservative manner throughout the campus, the architects played with more inventive ways to use this material at the new entrance and common. This concept is experienced in both the convex curving wall to the right of the entrance and the shallow vertical jack arch over the entry. A generous entry area provides ample protected space with seating for students to wait safely for after hours drop-off or pick-up.

The entrance experience at Kent extends from the parking lot to the front door. A serpentine brick wall links the two and provides a backdrop for a sculpture collection honoring the site's native creatures.

KENT DENVER SCHOOL COMMON

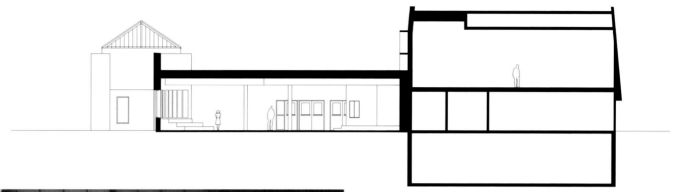

opposite left: Original main entrance
opposite right: Garden in front of student common
top: Section through common
bottom: View from main entrance to campus

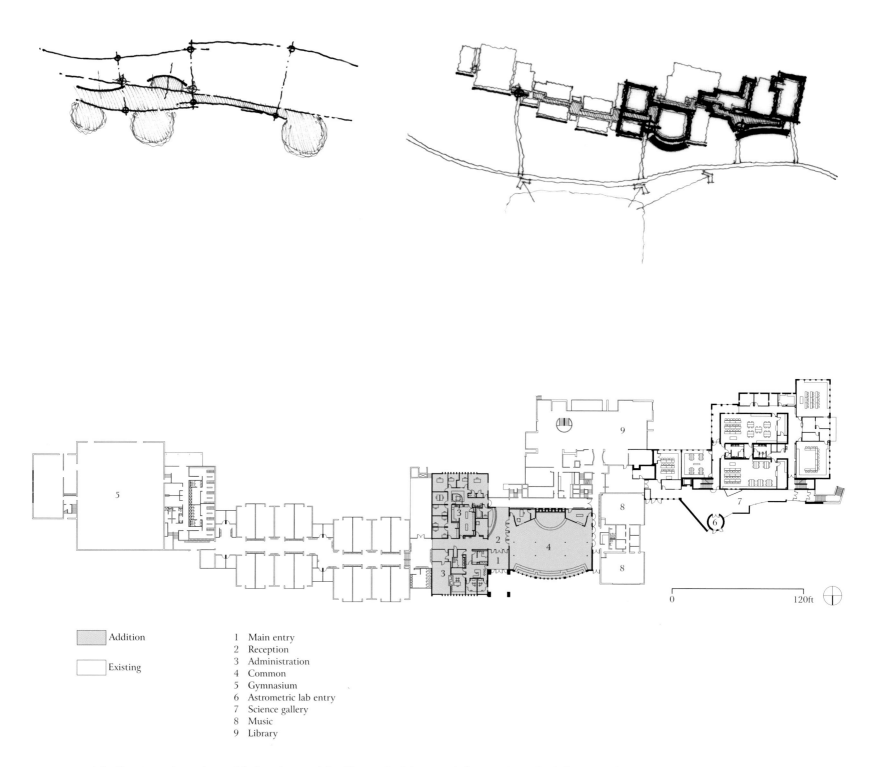

Addition
Existing

1 Main entry
2 Reception
3 Administration
4 Common
5 Gymnasium
6 Astrometric lab entry
7 Science gallery
8 Music
9 Library

0   120ft

top left: *Exterior paths, nodes, and hedges* | ***top right:*** *Upper school diagram* | ***bottom:*** *Main level floor plan* | ***opposite:*** *Music rehearsal in student common*
photography: *Greg Hursley; Paul Hutton (page 58 left)*

61

Kent Denver's Science and Technology Center offers a strong example of spaces designed for teaching. Kent's new center reinforces the school's role as a leader in secondary school science curriculum with features that include an electron microscope room, a genetic engineering lab, a center for innovation (dirty lab), and an astrometric lab. Classrooms are daylit with high-performance glazing and include dimmable pendant lights integrated with ceiling-mounted LCD projectors, teacher laptops, and wireless networking. The result is a high-tech hub of education.

The cylindrical tower of the astrometric lab serves as the main entry vestibule for the building. The architect had fun with the design of this space, incorporating an oculus at the top to let in an image of the sun, effectively creating a timepiece. Ten-second accuracy is achieved through the calibrated lines of latitude and longitude that wrap the wall. The image of the sun is at a tangent to the floor only at solar noon on the summer solstice, and at a tangent to the top of the wall only at solar noon on the winter solstice. The size of the space is therefore determined by the movement of the sun in the sky. This Stonehenge-like relationship imparts permanence to the structure and is used for teaching the fundamentals of astronomy.

KENT DENVER SCIENCE
AND TECHNOLOGY CENTER

Although designed with its own unique identity, the Science and Technology Center relates to the campus with its red brick and tan trim. The concave form of the adjoining science gallery plays on the convex wall of the nearby common, offering a yin–yang architectural composition. The use of curves extends further into the ringed signage band, engaging the sky and framing views of the heavens beyond.

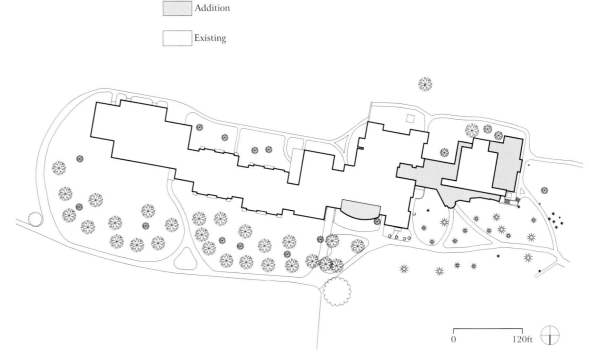

Addition

Existing

0   120ft

opposite: *Main entrance at sunset* | ***right:*** *Site plan*

top: Science/technology center with gallery
bottom: First level floor plan
opposite top: North elevation
opposite bottom: View of moon through entrance awning

1 Main entry
2 Reception
3 Administration
4 Common
5 Gymnasium
6 Astrometric lab entry
7 Science gallery
8 Music
9 Library

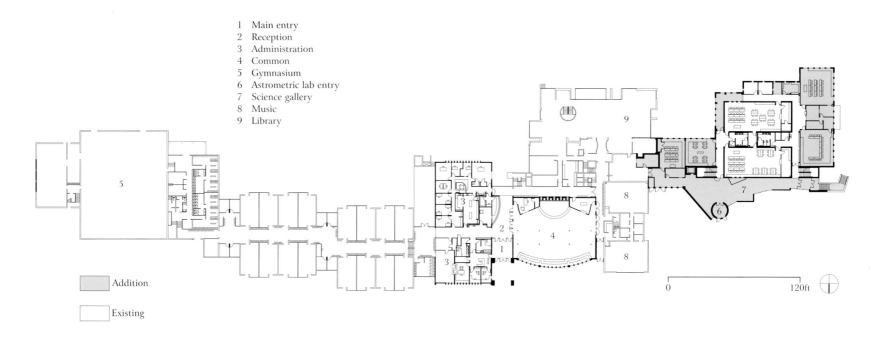

Addition

Existing

0   120ft

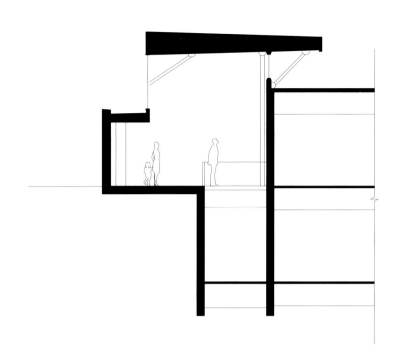

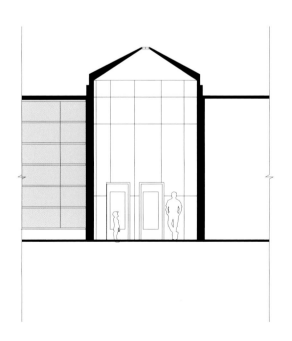

opposite: Sections through astrometric lab entry and gallery | **left:** *Science gallery*
above: *Astrometric lab at summer solstice showing sun at half-hour intervals* | ***photography:*** *Ron Pollard*

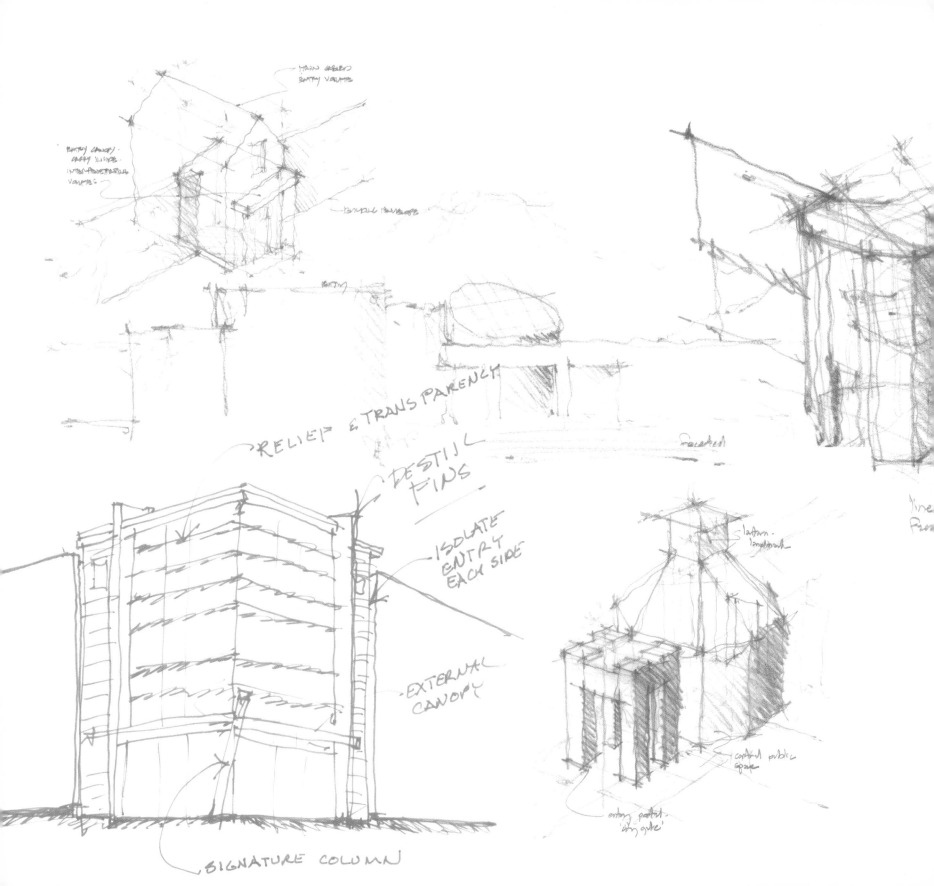

MAIN GROUND ENTRY VOLUME

ENTRY CANOPY CANOPY SLIDES INTERPENETRATES VOLUMES

BUILDING ENVELOPE

ENTRY

RELIEF & TRANSPARENCY

DESTIJL FINS

ISOLATE ENTRY EACH SIDE

EXTERNAL CANOPY

lantern landmark

central public space

entry portal 'city gate'

SIGNATURE COLUMN

2nd floor
landing and
balcony

OTHER SCHOOLS AND CAMPUSES

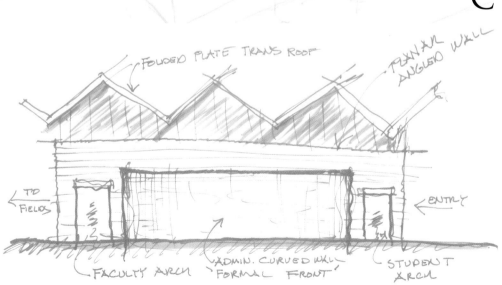

FOLDED PLATE TRANS ROOF

PLANAR ANGLED WALL

TO FIELDS

ENTRY

FACULTY ARCH

ADMIN. CURVED WALL
'FORMAL FRONT'

STUDENT ARCH

This 5000-square-foot office building for a local school district is located in a rural community on Colorado's eastern plains. The design incorporates elements from the surrounding farm structures such as the projected end eaves, a cupola, and board-and-batten siding. The main entrance faces a highway, which is the primary entrance to the town of Ault. As a result, the administration building greets visitors, shaping their first impression of this agricultural community.

The project was built on a modest budget and required careful use of dollars available. Brick was used on the principal entrance façade to provide a formal public front, while economical board-and-batten concrete-based siding, consistent with the rural setting, was chosen for the remaining walls. The highway elevation is defined by projecting brick piers that provide a sense of rhythm for anyone driving or walking by the building. The entrance projects outward to receive visitors and is defined by a cupola structure above. Once inside the lobby, the cupola provides a dramatic spatial experience and helps to organize the simple circulation system. The volume and natural light created by the cupola also provide an interior sense of entry to the boardroom and offices beyond. The reception area, boardroom, and the two primary hallways all originate at the cupola.

Each office has a generous amount of windows, providing non-glare natural light and allowing the electric light fixtures to remain off most of the time. The boardroom, designed to host school district board meetings, has become a community meeting room that also accommodates a wide variety of the town's needs.

top: North elevation | *bottom:* Building at sunrise | *opposite:* Entry detail

Procession, Identity

AULT ADMINISTRATION BUILDING

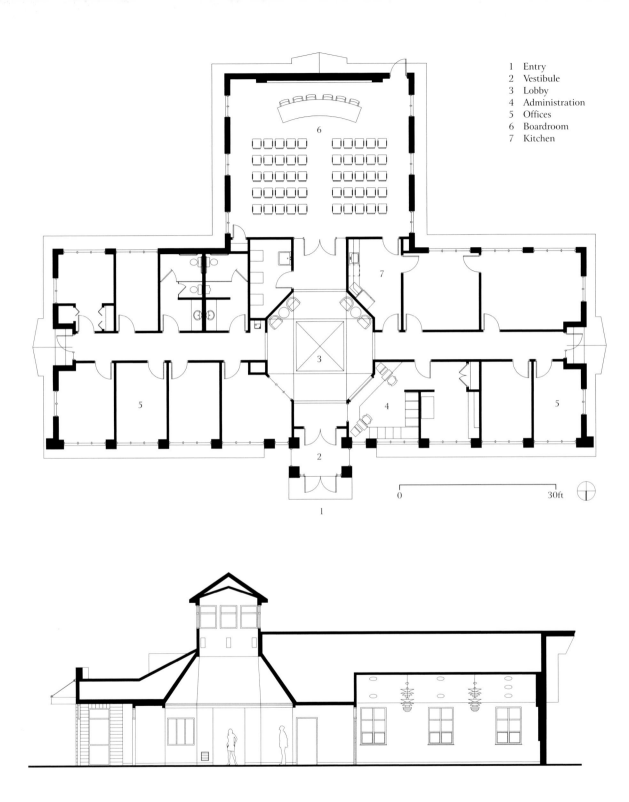

1 Entry
2 Vestibule
3 Lobby
4 Administration
5 Offices
6 Boardroom
7 Kitchen

0 _____ 30ft

top: Floor plan | *bottom:* Section through entry, lobby, and boardroom | *opposite:* View from main street

top: East façade looking back toward street | *bottom:* Section through boardroom
opposite top: Main entrance *opposite bottom left:* Detail above entrance doors
opposite bottom right: East elevation

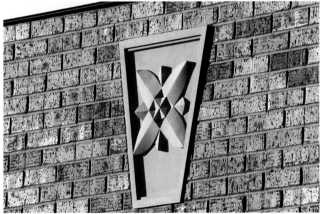

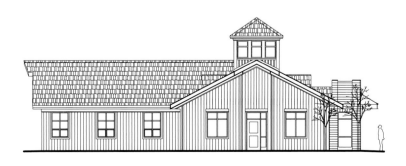

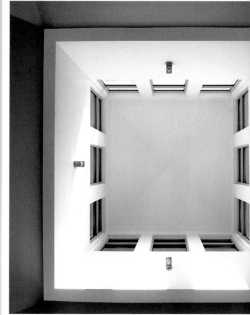

The Chinese Children Adoption International Cultural Center is the world's largest placement agency for orphaned Chinese children. When the organization called for an addition, a two-story atrium space was added to accommodate a new elevator, provide a lobby sitting area, and a second floor overlook with views of the adjacent open space.

The existing center looked like a typical 1980's office building. The architects wanted to incorporate Asian-influenced elements into the addition to give the center a distinctive identity and reflect the activities going on inside. The new back entrance features transparent walls topped by a dominant roof form along with a traditional Chinese arch-shaped window at the entrance doors. The horizontal detailing winds its way skyward to suggest the lofty charge of the organization.

The glass curtain wall, polished granite, and steel/glass staircase all provide an open quality to the entry. The second-floor overlook affords views of the greenbelt and playground, and high-performance glass prevents glare while minimizing heat gain and loss.

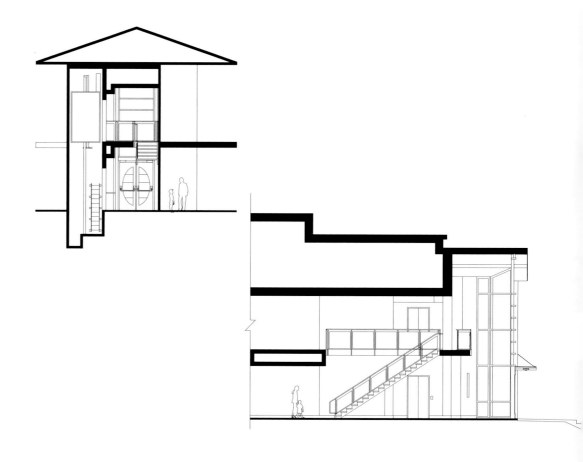

CHINESE CHILDREN ADOPTION INTERNATIONAL CULTURAL CENTER

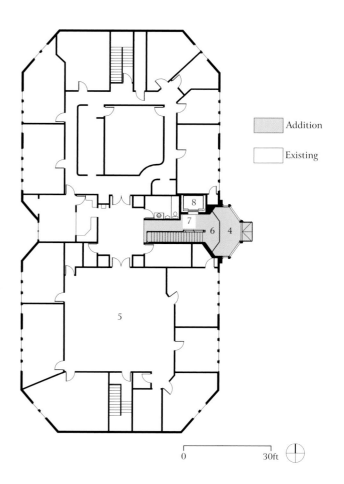

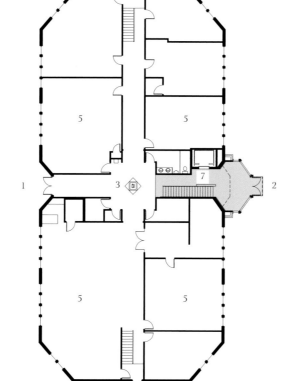

Addition

Existing

1 Existing main entrance
2 New rear entry
3 Lobby
4 Lobby below
5 Office area
6 Balcony overlook
7 New stair
8 New elevator

0   30ft

opposite top left: Second level lobby looking out to greenbelt
opposite top middle: East elevation | *opposite top right:* Entry from playground
opposite bottom left: First level floor plan *opposite bottom right:* Second level floor plan
top left and top right: Entry from playground | *bottom:* North elevation
photography: Alan Ford

The Denver Arts and Technology Academy is in and of the city. Sitting on a gritty and tight one-acre lot, the three-story school is punctuated by an entry featuring a dynamic two-story, floor-to-ceiling glass lobby. A library is situated prominently on the third floor of the entry element.

With its subtle De Stijl-like design, the entrance became the school's primary architectural feature. While the entrance faces a busy city street, its western orientation offers scenic views of a park and the snow-capped Rocky Mountain range beyond. The rest of the architectural details are a function of the activities inside. High-efficiency lighting and sloped ceilings were designed for the classrooms. Each classroom has one large center window and two narrower side windows. Together, and by virtue of their height, they provide abundant daylight throughout the building.

The building sits as close to the sidewalk and street as possible, to reinforce the definition of the urban street. Trees were planted along the sidewalk to further develop this concept. In contrast to the solid appearance of the masonry elements, the entrance piece is very open and light; its transparency invites sidewalk views of the lobby mural by well-known western artist Manuel Martinez.

left: Entrance view from adjacent park | *right: Section through entrance*
opposite top: Main entrance at sunset | *opposite bottom: West elevation*

DENVER ARTS AND TECHNOLOGY ACADEMY

83

*left: Site plan | **right, top to bottom:** Third level floor plan; second level floor plan; first level floor plan*
opposite: *Lobby with custom mural by artist Manuel Martinez | **photography:** Ed LaCasse*

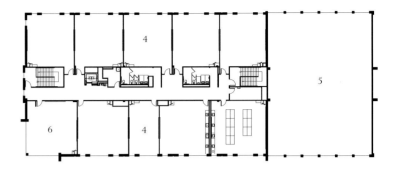

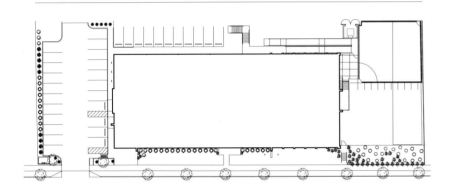

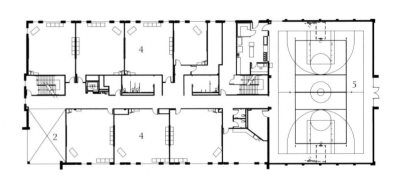

1 Entry
2 Lobby
3 Administration
4 Classrooms
5 Multipurpose room
6 Library

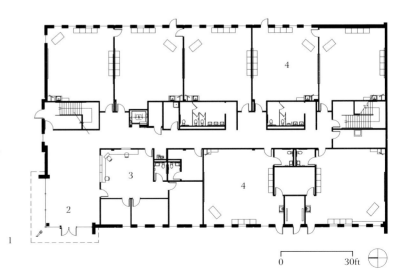

0   30ft

The renovation and addition for Drake Middle School required most of the existing building to be completely gutted to bring it up to the school's educational specifications. The client initially considered completely demolishing the building but, under the architect's guidance, decided instead to work with the sophisticated underlying geometry of the original design to strategically add an administration area, eight classrooms, a library, and a new entrance.

A primary objective of the renovation was to give the entry a singular focus. "An entrance should be uplifting, never mundane," explains Alan Ford, design principal. "You need to see it from the street—and just as important, the entry should indicate what's inside."

Punctuated by a band of yellow brick, the entrance design is playful and creative, integrating the yellow spandrels that run the length of the original building. A glazed brick opening in front of the principal's window was customized for unobstructed views of the entry area. An additional nod to the yellow brick is also picked up in the steel struts above the entrance, creating a punch of unexpected color and making this most unusual form the brightest spot on the building.

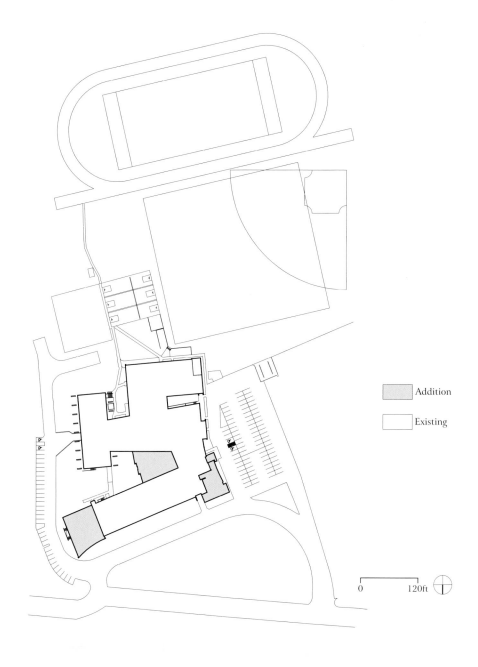

Addition

Existing

0   120ft

D R A K E   M I D D L E   S C H O O L

Addition

Existing

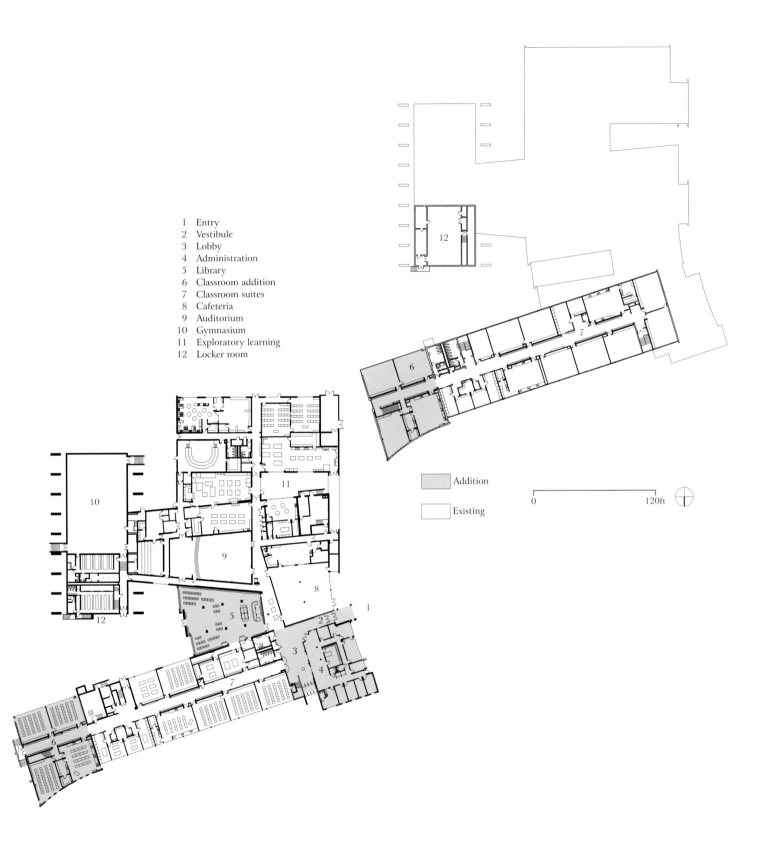

1   Entry
2   Vestibule
3   Lobby
4   Administration
5   Library
6   Classroom addition
7   Classroom suites
8   Cafeteria
9   Auditorium
10 Gymnasium
11 Exploratory learning
12 Locker room

Addition

Existing

0   120ft

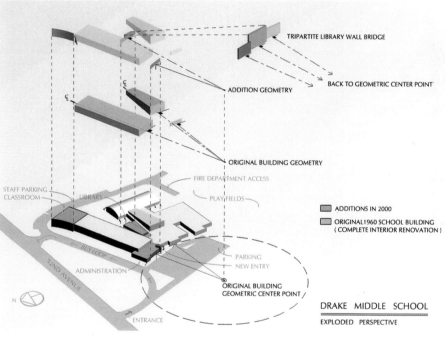

TRIPARTITE LIBRARY WALL BRIDGE

BACK TO GEOMETRIC CENTER POINT

ADDITION GEOMETRY

ORIGINAL BUILDING GEOMETRY

STAFF PARKING
CLASSROOM

LIBRARY

FIRE DEPARTMENT ACCESS

PLAY FIELDS

ADDITIONS IN 2000

ORIGINAL 1960 SCHOOL BUILDING
(COMPLETE INTERIOR RENOVATION)

BUS LOOP

52ND AVENUE

ADMINISTRATION

PARKING

NEW ENTRY

ORIGINAL BUILDING
GEOMETRIC CENTER POINT

N

ENTRANCE

DRAKE MIDDLE SCHOOL

EXPLODED PERSPECTIVE

opposite left: First level floor plan | *opposite right:* Second level floor plan
left: Curved wall of classroom addition | *above:* Exploded perspective illustrating building geometry

The original entrance to Green Mountain Elementary School featured a 1960's era nondescript door that was challenging to locate and far from inviting. The design was updated with new administrative offices, entry, and lobby. The architects focused on creating an entrance statement from the school's two street views. The dynamic curve of the new administration area becomes a formal welcoming gesture to Union Boulevard—the public face of the building—and frees the existing structure for more educational spaces. The addition also provides a means of controlling access to the administrative area by creating two distinctive zones. Now visitors entering the lobby are able to interact with administrators, but are buffered from the actual offices.

A folded plate roof cuts across the building at an angle, running parallel to Union Boulevard. The addition of this saw-tooth form offers a seamless integration with the existing folded plate above the cafeteria and gymnasium, enhancing the original design and defining the pathway from the main entrance through to the athletic fields and playground. Sitting high atop the school, like a range of mountain peaks, the form's subtle movement seems to beckon to the arriving cars and buses, as if waving them onto the campus.

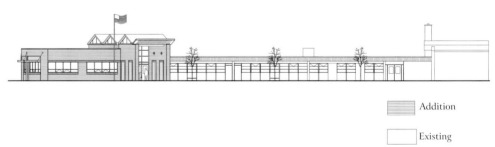

Addition

Existing

GREEN MOUNTAIN ELEMENTARY SCHOOL

opposite top: View from street | *opposite bottom:* North elevation | *above:* Entrance at beginning of day

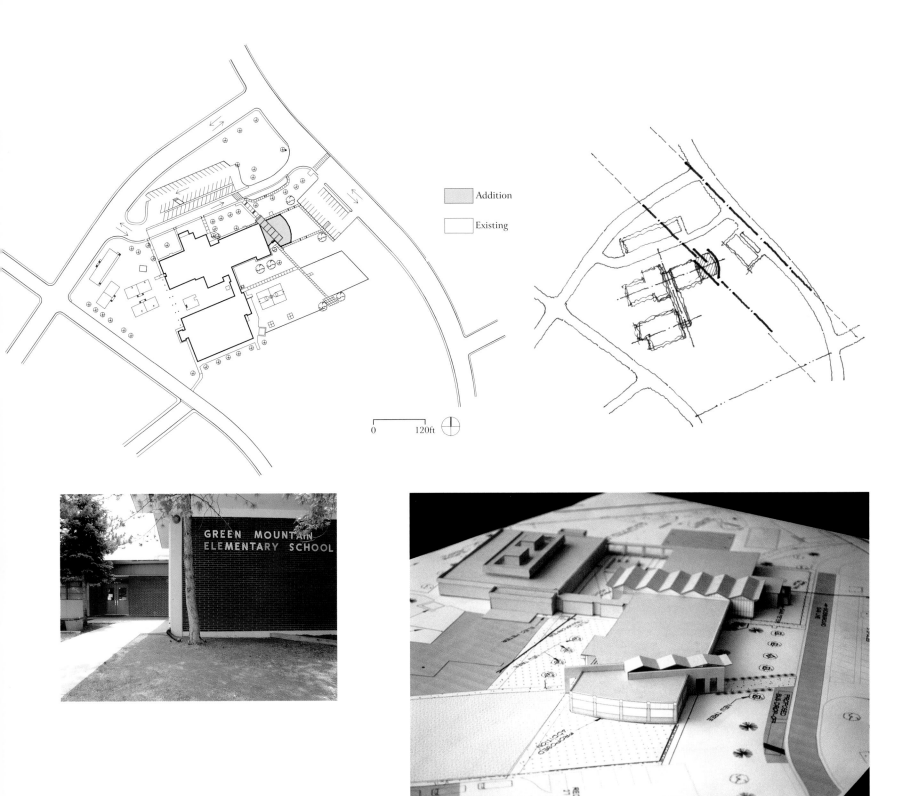

Addition

Existing

0   120ft

GREEN MOUNTAIN
ELEMENTARY SCHOOL

opposite: New main entry detail | *left*: Rear entry from parking lot | *right*: Rear entry from courtyard

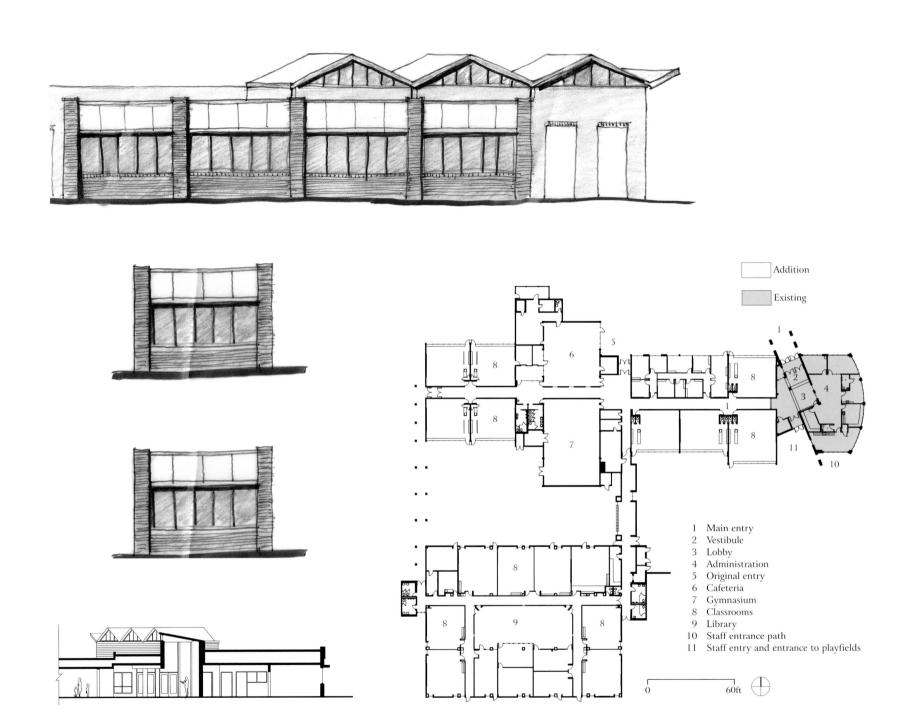

top: Study of entry | *middle left*: Concept studies of administration wall | *bottom left*: Section through lobby interior | *right*: First level floor plan
opposite left: Entry lobby | *opposite right*: Section through lobby | *photography*: Greg Hursley (pages 96,100,103); Matt Slater (pages 97,99); Alan Ford (pages 98,101)

Addition
Existing

1 Main entry
2 Vestibule
3 Lobby
4 Administration
5 Original entry
6 Cafeteria
7 Gymnasium
8 Classrooms
9 Library
10 Staff entrance path
11 Staff entry and entrance to playfields

0   60ft

Housing a special education program for children with emotional and behavioral problems, the Joliet Center provides a transitional learning opportunity for students in grades six through twelve. The center operated from a series of modular buildings for several years and felt a bit like a mobile home park, lacking a sense of stability so important for this particular group of students.

The new building influences the children positively by developing a sense of calm through the design. Classrooms are grouped in three separate single-loaded wings, to minimize congestion and simplify wayfinding. The school's intimate scale offers a comforting residential character, integrating the building into its surrounding neighborhood of single-family dwellings and making the children feel, quite simply, at home. Each space is 100 percent daylit, minimizing the use of electric light and connecting the students with the outside world at every turn.

The small, 2.5-acre site results in the building entrance being very close to the street. The high gable roof of the lobby represents a nurturing, familiar form to further emphasize the residential feel of the architecture. This roof form is echoed in the rooftop mechanical system enclosures. A whimsical angled canopy above the front door acknowledges the south side approach and welcomes the students into the school's warm embrace.

top: East elevation | *bottom:* View from driveway | *opposite left:* Detail at front door
opposite right: Laser-cut building and site model | *opposite bottom:* West elevation

JOLIET LEARNING CENTER

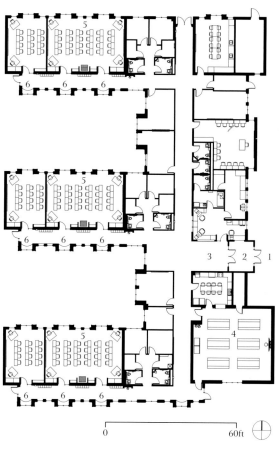

1   Entry
2   Vestibule
3   Lobby/reception
4   Multipurpose room
5   Classroom
6   Window seat

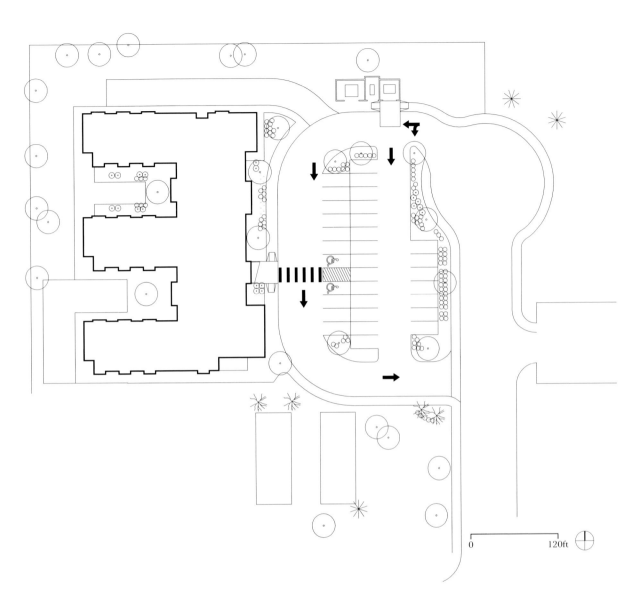

opposite top: Site plan | *opposite bottom:* View from athletic field | *top left:* Courtyard | *top right:* Window seat at corridor | *bottom:* Building section

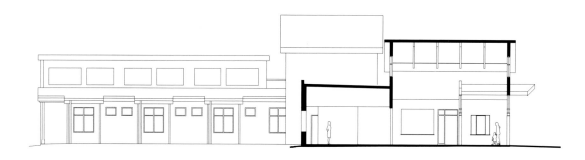

opposite: *Lobby with reception desk* | ***top:*** *Section through multipurpose room* | ***bottom left:*** *Multipurpose room* | ***bottom right:*** *Typical classroom*
photography: *Ed LaCasse*

Hutton Ford Architects' 1993 addition to Lyons Elementary included a library with an exterior light shelf for daylighting the interior. The light shelf extended over the front doors (see before image) forming an entry canopy. When the owner requested additional improvements to the school in 2004 the architects incorporated a new signature entry.

Nestled in the foothills of the Rocky Mountains, the town of Lyons, Colorado is famous for providing beautiful pink sandstone to cities across the country. It seemed only natural to incorporate this local material into the new entrance design of Lyons Elementary School. Set back from the street, the school's entrance forms a large "L" shape; the trademark pinkish Lyons sandstone is used here as a veneer.

The raised form that includes the L provides shelter from the weather, and is high enough to be seen easily from the street and parking lot. A large glazed area within the L brings light deep inside the building.

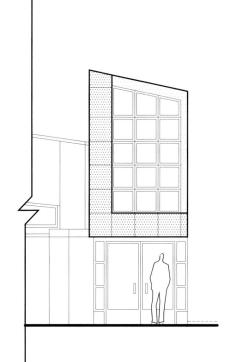

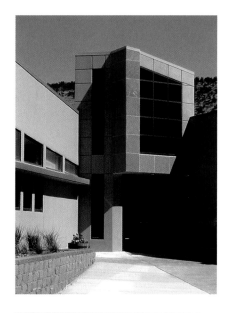

L Y O N S   E L E M E N T A R Y   S C H O O L

opposite left: Elevation | *opposite top right:* Detail of new entry | *opposite bottom right:* Entry before | *above:* Overview of new main entrance

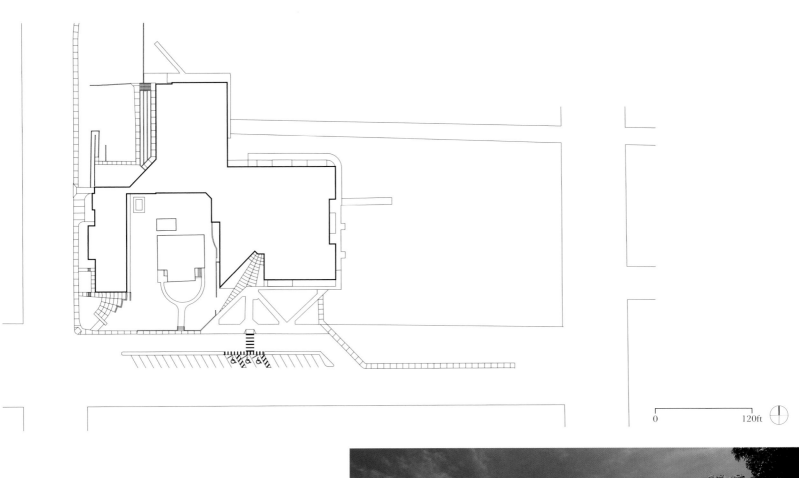

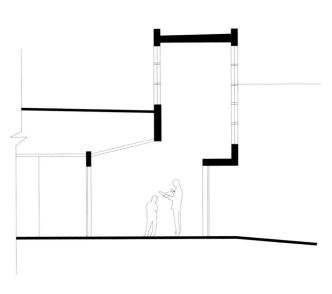

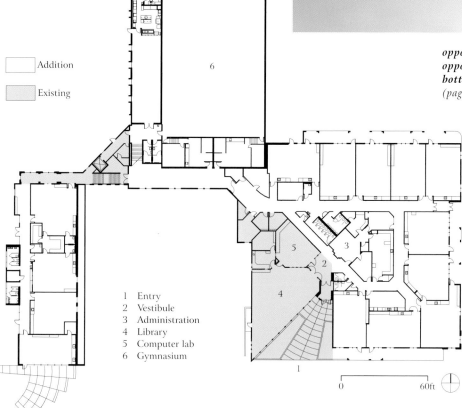

Addition

Existing

opposite top: Site plan | opposite bottom left: Section through entry
opposite bottom right: Front view of entry | top: Interior view of entrance
bottom: Floor plan | photography: Paul Hutton (page 112); Alan Ford
(pages 113–115)

1 Entry
2 Vestibule
3 Administration
4 Library
5 Computer lab
6 Gymnasium

0   60ft

The original entrance of the Lyons Middle/Senior High School was hidden in a large recess and nearly invisible. The school's renovation and expansion features a bold entry area that connects to a new common. This common is located between the old exterior wall and the addition, creating a link between the main entrance on the north that serves the bus loop and visitor's parking lot, and the back entrance on the south that serves the student parking lot.

The common provides access to both the gymnasium and cafetorium (cafeteria and auditorium combined), and is capped by a translucent skylight. This commons becomes an organizer—a wayfinding element—for the building.

The main entrance is held in place by a screen wall that becomes the front façade. It is hexagonal in shape to reflect the geometry of the adjacent cafetorium and stage, and is again capped by translucent material, keeping the interior entrance space open and bright.

LYONS MIDDLE/SENIOR HIGH SCHOOL

__opposite:__ New entry and addition | __top:__ Detail of translucent roof at entrance | __bottom:__ East elevation

117

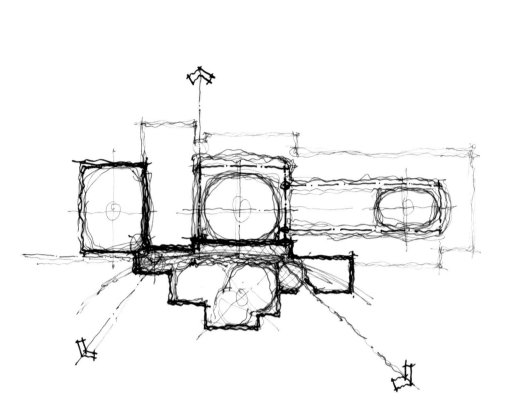

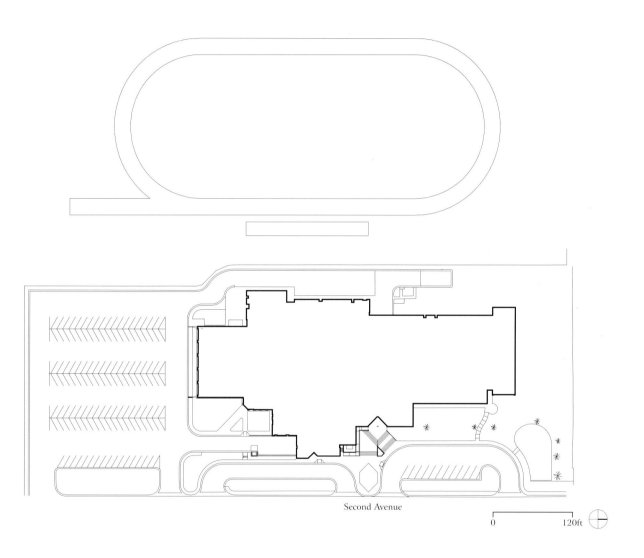

opposite top left: Conceptual diagram | ***opposite top right:*** *Secondary entrance from playfields*
opposite bottom: *New east façade* | ***above:*** *Site plan*

Second Avenue

0   120ft

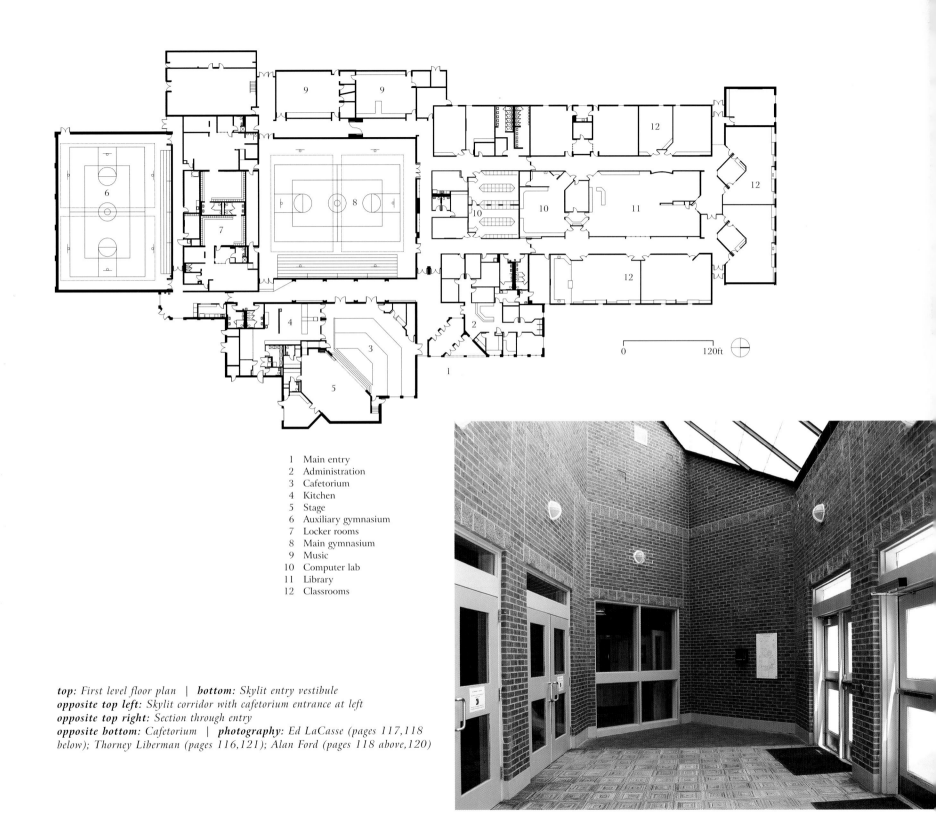

1   Main entry
2   Administration
3   Cafetorium
4   Kitchen
5   Stage
6   Auxiliary gymnasium
7   Locker rooms
8   Main gymnasium
9   Music
10 Computer lab
11 Library
12 Classrooms

top: First level floor plan | *bottom*: Skylit entry vestibule
opposite top left: Skylit corridor with cafetorium entrance at left
opposite top right: Section through entry
opposite bottom: Cafetorium | *photography*: Ed LaCasse (pages 117,118
below); Thorney Liberman (pages 116,121); Alan Ford (pages 118 above,120)

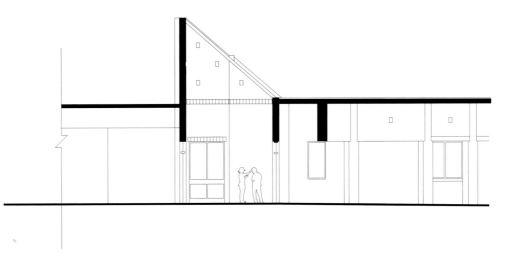

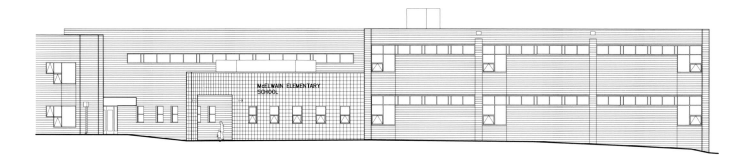

In contrast to the lofty forms that have become the hallmark of Hutton Ford entry design, the McElwain Elementary School entrance is shorter than the rest of the building. It curves to fuse the old and new portions of the renovated school, which are at a 45-degree angle to one another.

The entire entrance experience is organized by a straight line that starts at the street, proceeds through the front doors and right out the back doors. Along this line are a landscaped plaza, the flagpole, the vestibule, the two-story lobby, and the playground.

The architects incorporated 12-inch square wall tiles from the original design into the new entry, giving the entrance a punch of color and providing contrast with the brick classroom wings. The daylit atrium lobby welcomes those who enter and an internal bridge enlivens the space further. Transparency is key here, as the design provides unobstructed views from the front of the building to the back, and vice versa. Views from the lobby open to the playground, street, trees, and sky beyond.

top: South elevation | *bottom:* Street view of entrance
opposite: View of entry arch from bus drop-off

M C E L W A I N   E L E M E N T A R Y   S C H O O L

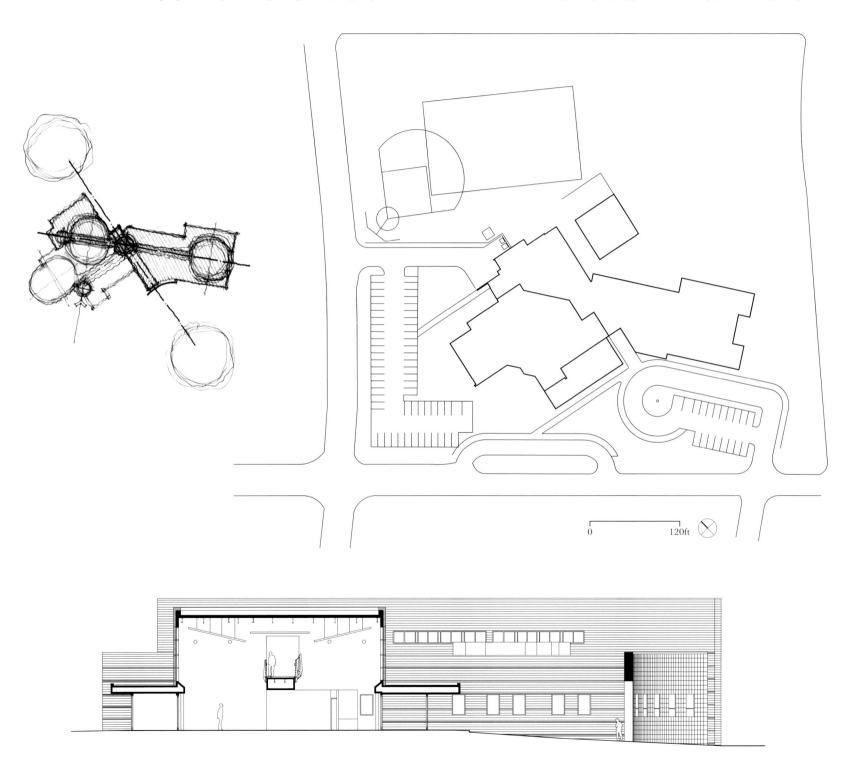

top left: Conceptual design diagram | *top right:* Site plan | *bottom:* Section through lobby | *opposite:* Detail of free-standing entry arch

0   120ft

above: Main entry detail | *right:* Lobby entry from playfields

An extensive renovation/addition project for Pine Lane Elementary School did not include any changes to the entrance. The architects, however, injected a bit of creativity and community involvement into the design process, commissioning a competition that invited local artists to share how they would use sculpture or art as an identifying form.

Motivated by the name of the school, as well as its location on Pine Lane, the winning design was an abstract representation of a ponderosa pine and the hills beyond. The eclectic sculpture uses multiple layers and various natural and hand-painted metals to create a canopy over the entrance. The image of a ponderosa pine is repeated as a red pattern in the adjoining pavement, leading children up the sidewalk and into the building. A vertical brick pier was also added to lead visitors from the remote parking lot to the main entrance.

The compelling inspiration for the new entrance brought a depth of character to the redesigned Pine Lane Elementary School. Students, staff, and parents who enter the building now have a greater appreciation for the significant investment made by the school district on their behalf.

PINE LANE ELEMENTARY SCHOOL

left: New main entry with artist-designed canopy
right: Abstracted pine tree in pavement

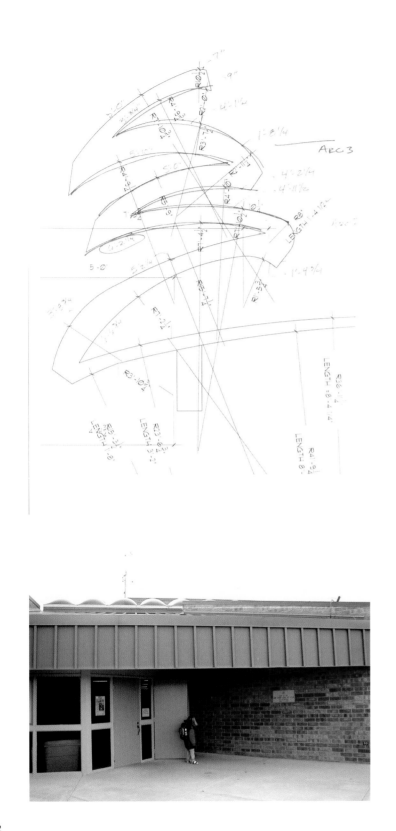

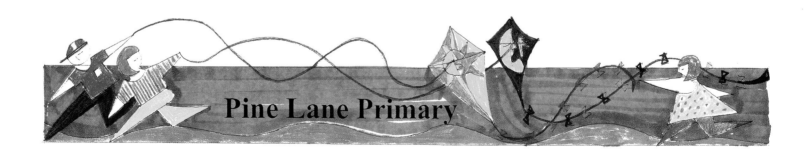

opposite top left: *Construction drawing of metal pine tree* | ***opposite bottom left:*** *Original entrance* | ***opposite right:*** *Detail of abstracted pine tree*
above: *Artist's concept drawings* | ***photography:*** *Fred Furmeister; Paul Hutton (page 132 left)*

Located on the University of Denver campus, the Ricks Center for Gifted Children provides opportunities for students from 3 to 13 years old to develop their leadership potential, learn the value of cooperation, and excel at their own individual pace.

The architecture is loosely derived from the traditional buildings that make up the university campus, including red brick and active roofscapes. The Ricks Center was specifically designed to not look like a traditional school, but to appear as an alternative and progressive educational venue. Here, the sloped roof engages the sky as the building's angles point to significant campus landmarks. The geometric patterns incorporated in the façades were developed in an effort to appeal to the children attending the Ricks Center, some of whom might also be taking college-level mathematics courses at the university.

The emphasis on wayfinding and pattern extends throughout the building's interior. The entire circulation system is covered in a 12-inch square tile floor with a five-color pattern based on a fractal mathematical algorithm specifically developed for the school. Students play games using this pattern and can use its properties in their math classes. The hallway is shaped and modulated to provide additional spaces for impromptu educational activities.

RICKS CENTER FOR GIFTED CHILDREN

Above: *West elevation from street*

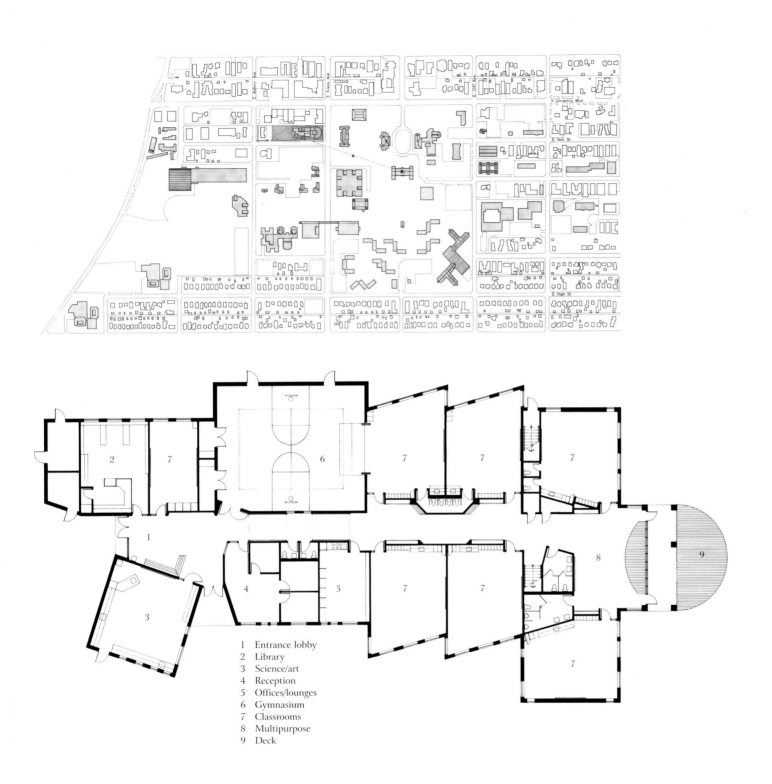

1 Entrance lobby
2 Library
3 Science/art
4 Reception
5 Offices/lounges
6 Gymnasium
7 Classrooms
8 Multipurpose
9 Deck

top: Campus plan | *bottom:* Floor plan | *opposite:* Night view of recessed main entrance

opposite: Main corridor with fractal floor pattern | *left:* Daylit multipurpose space | *right:* Daylit science room | *photography:* Andrew Kramer

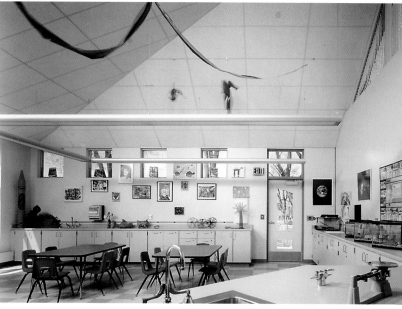

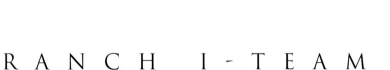

Ranch I-Team serves a select group of high school students who are not succeeding in the typical large-school environment. This alternative educational program provides a small-group setting that often takes an expeditionary approach to learning. Working to define the school's ranch-like identity, Hutton Ford employed a rich material palette, combining masonry elements and warm colors to evoke a sense of familiarity in the design.

The entrance is located very close to the parking lot but away from the street, a decision made to accommodate the majority of students who drive to school. The architects' primary focus was to give the entrance a sense of height and impact, making it stand out and announce itself upon approach. The tower form helps to emphasize the entry, while a canopy juts out to offer protection from inclement weather.

The soft glow of translucent material above the entrance serves as a beacon, drawing the kids in with a keen sensitivity to the school's mission.

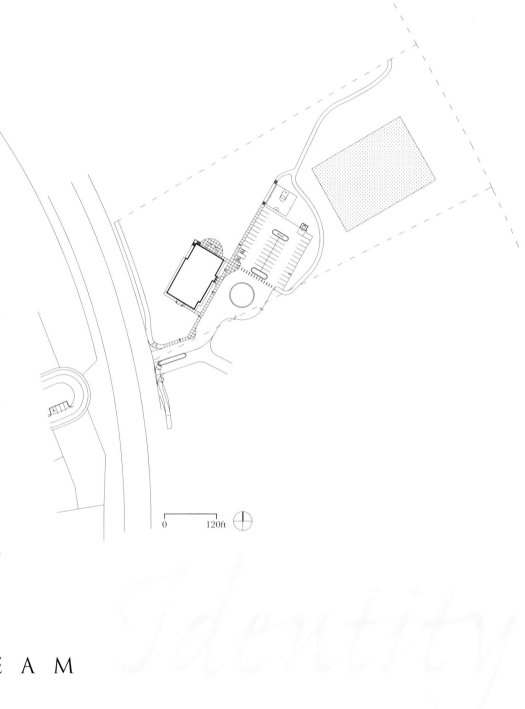

0   120ft

RANCH I-TEAM

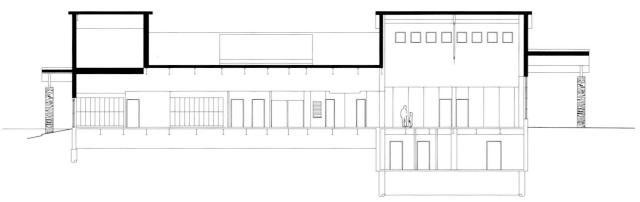

top: View from northeast | *bottom:* North elevation
opposite top: View from southeast | *opposite bottom:* East elevation

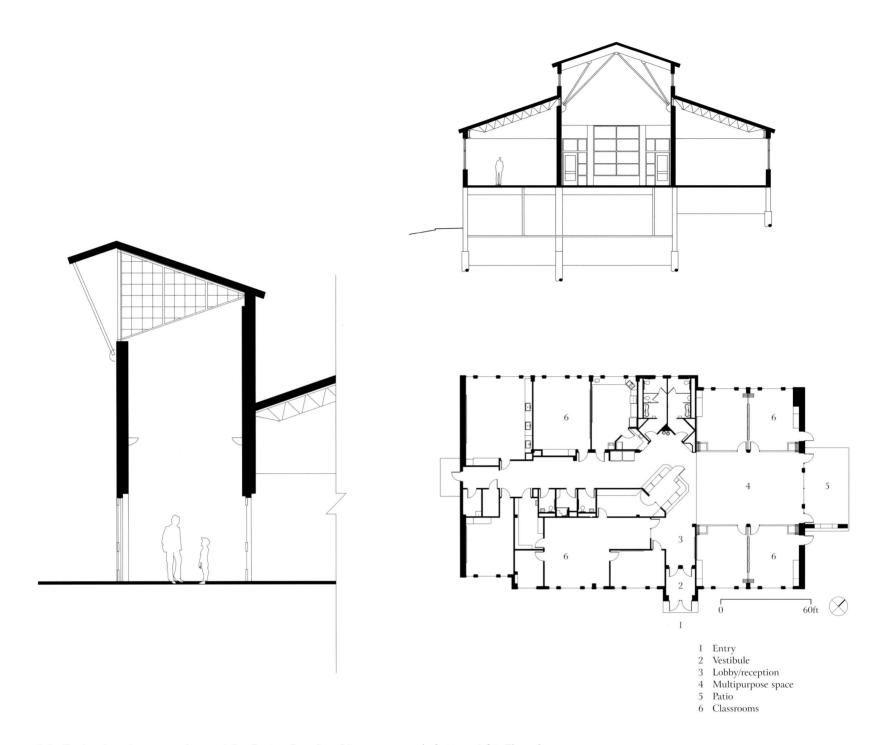

1   Entry
2   Vestibule
3   Lobby/reception
4   Multipurpose space
5   Patio
6   Classrooms

left: Section through entrance | *top right:* Section through multipurpose space | *bottom right:* Floor plan
opposite: Multipurpose space | *photography:* Ed LaCasse (pages 141,142); Ron Johnson (pages 143,145)

The Rocky Mountain School of Expeditionary Learning (RMSEL) is an innovative program founded on the ideals of Outward Bound, with the curriculum organized around multidisciplinary learning expeditions. RMSEL is located in a former elementary school building that had been abandoned and was in desperate need of a facelift.

To give the school new life, the two oldest portions of the existing building were demolished and a large new masonry screen wall was constructed to cover the opening. This wall faces the busy street, with large windows designed to reveal some of the activity going on inside the school.

A dramatic new elevator tower and entry vestibule anchor the new entrance, improving internal accessibility while enhancing the school's outward visibility. The unusual brick patterning was inspired by existing elements found on one portion of the school, while the tall, heavily textured wall alludes to the rock-climbing adventures encountered by the students as a part of their expeditionary learning experiences. Tension cables, reminiscent of climbing ropes, support the new canopy and reinforce the school's identity.

R O C K Y   M O U N T A I N   S C H O O L   O F   E X P E D I T I O N A R Y   L E A R N I N G

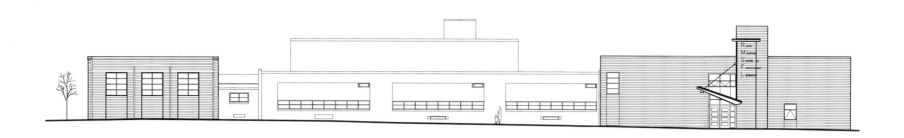

opposite left: Main entry with elevator tower | *opposite right:* View to street | *top:* South elevation
bottom left: Entry vestibule with translucent glazed canopy | *bottom right:* Elevator tower

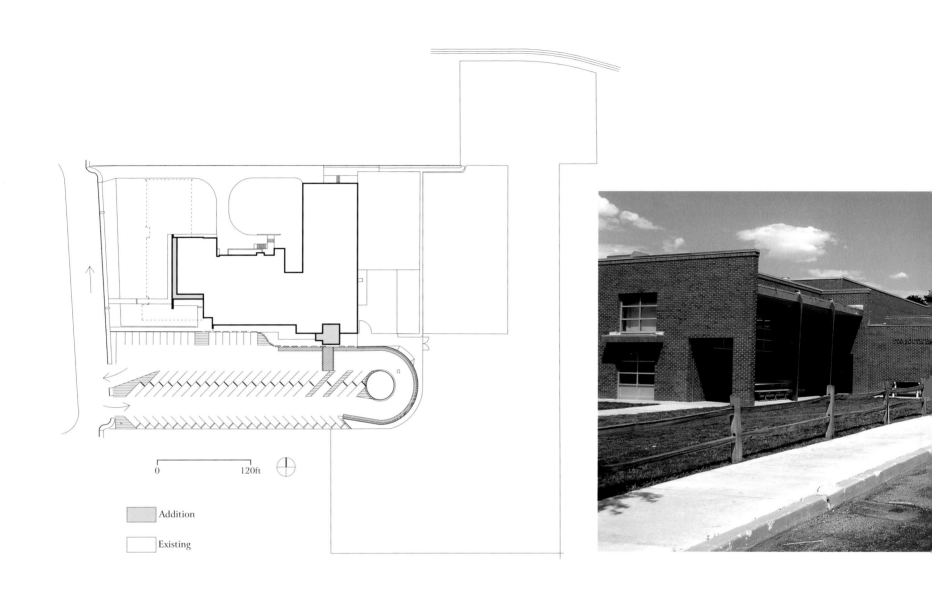

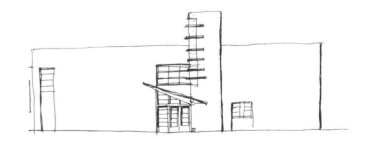

left: Site plan | *top right*: Entry tower from street | *bottom right*: Entry elevation study
opposite top: First level floor plan | *opposite bottom*: Entry elevation studies

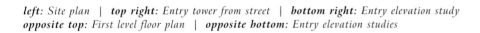

0   120ft

Addition

Existing

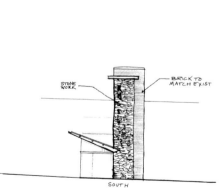

STONE WORK

BRICK TO MATCH EXIST

SOUTH

WEST

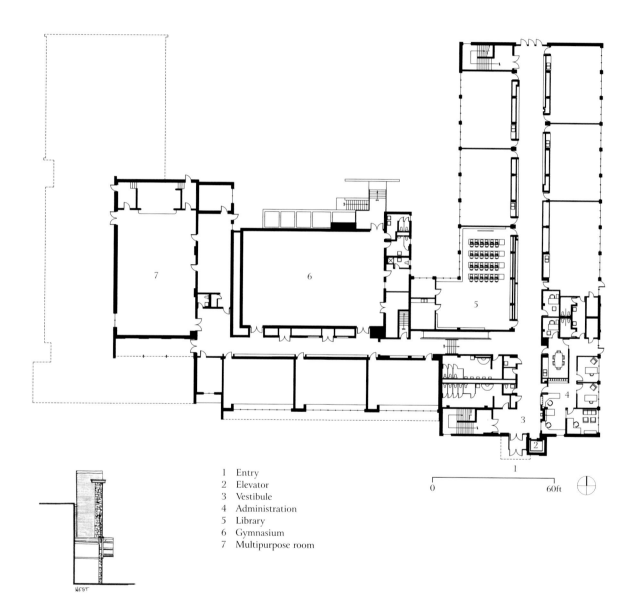

1 Entry
2 Elevator
3 Vestibule
4 Administration
5 Library
6 Gymnasium
7 Multipurpose room

0   60ft

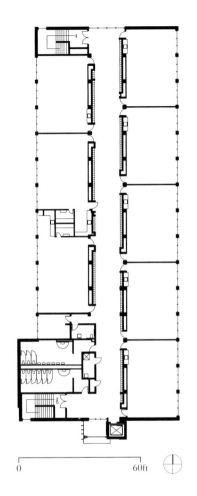

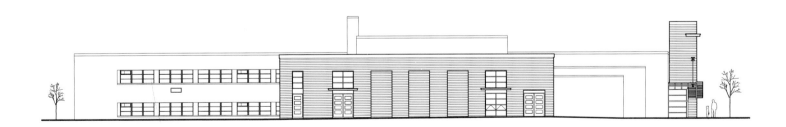

top left: Second level floor plan | *top right*: New west façade fronting the main street | *bottom*: West elevation | *opposite top*: Detail of west façade
opposite bottom: New west façade | *photography*: Alan Ford

The Stargate Charter School, one of the first of its kind in Colorado, is specifically geared for gifted students. Housed in an old shopping center for 10 years, the Stargate community craved a new facility more reflective of its mission.

"In this age where schools so often feel like factories for learning, we thought it appropriate to make this school a temple for learning instead," said Paul Hutton, design principal. His hybrid design features a classic Greek temple form rising from the center of traditional red concrete-block classroom wings. This powerful juxtaposition of styles makes a grand statement and serves to express the school's strong standing in the community.

The classroom blocks face two main streets, where a stately tower announces the entrance. The canopy— a distinctive Hutton Ford entry element—provides protection from the weather and is visible from both streets and all parking spaces. The entry imparts a residential flavor, connecting the school to its suburban location. Inside, just beyond the tower, the lobby ceiling features a star field of the northern hemisphere. This homage to the night sky ties into the school's identity. Constellations are precisely mapped and fiber-optically lit, with each star's brightness accurately represented in three magnitudes. Families were invited to purchase stars in honor of their children, enabling the school to raise thousands of dollars through this one-of-a-kind fundraiser.

STARGATE CHARTER SCHOOL

opposite: *Main entry with bus drop-off in foreground* | ***top:*** *South elevation* | ***bottom:*** *View from the main street*

0   120ft

0   60ft

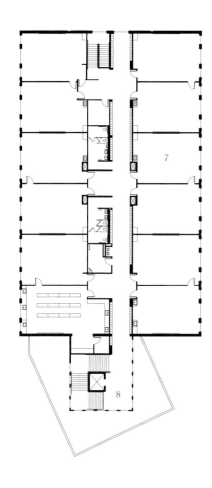

1 Entry
2 Vestibule
3 Lobby/reception with "star field" display
4 Administration
5 Multipurpose space
6 Library
7 Classrooms
8 Vertical circulation lobby

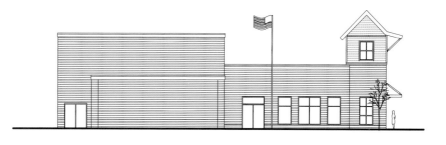

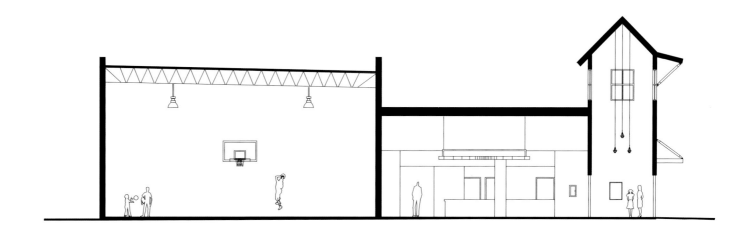

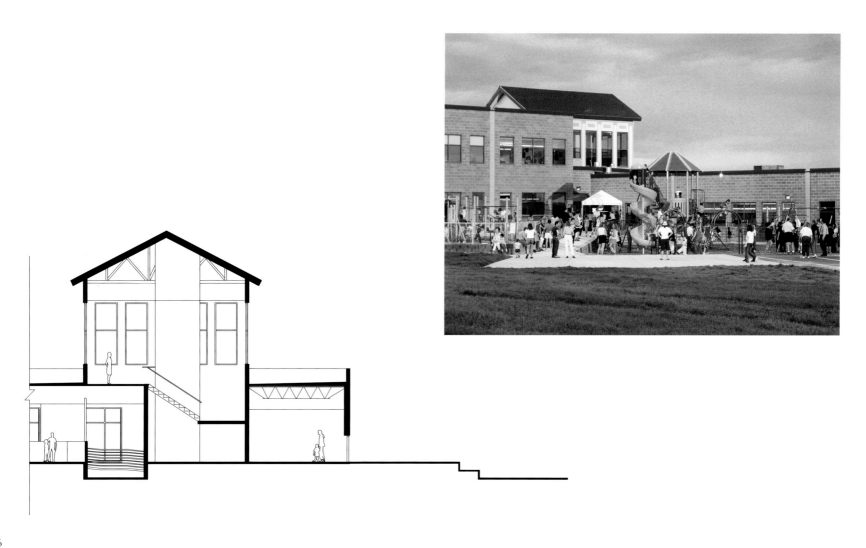

opposite top: Section through entrance, lobby, and gymnasium | opposite middle: Playground
opposite bottom: Section through two-story "temple" space | left: Installation of star field at lobby
right: Entry looking up | photography: Ed LaCasse

Alan Ford, AIA, is a principal with Hutton Ford Architects P.C. He has designed more than 75 K–12 school projects and is author of the book *Designing the Sustainable School*. A licensed architect with 28 years of experience, Alan has a Bachelor of Environmental Design and Master of Architecture from the University of Colorado. Prior to forming Hutton Ford Architects with Paul Hutton in 1993, he worked with architectural firms W.C. Muchow & Partners in Colorado, Kohn Pedersen Fox Architects in New York, and John Burgee Architects with Philip Johnson, New York. Alan also served as an honorarium professor and guest critic at the University of Colorado School of Architecture.

ALAN FORD, AIA

Paul Hutton, AIA, is a principal with Hutton Ford Architects P.C. He has designed more than 90 K–12 school projects. A licensed architect with 28 years of experience, Paul has a Bachelor of Arts from Princeton University and a Masters Degree in Architecture and Environmental Planning from the University of Virginia. Prior to forming Hutton Ford Architects with Alan Ford in 1993, he worked with architectural firms W.C. Muchow & Partners in Colorado, Lerner | Ladds + Bartels in Rhode Island, and Estudio Fernandez-Santamaria in Spain. Paul has also been an honorarium professor at the University of Colorado School of Architecture since 1997 where he has taught Construction Documents and Fundamentals of Daylighting.

JENNIFER SEWARD

Jennifer Seward is editor-in-chief of *Architect Colorado*. Her work has been featured in various regional publications for the built environment. She lives in Denver, Colorado, with her husband and two children, and she has endeavored to create a sense of entry in the multiple homes she has remodeled.

PAUL HUTTON, AIA

ACKNOWLEDGMENTS

We would like to thank Paul Latham and Alessina Brooks of The Images Publishing Group for their wisdom and insight throughout the development of this book. Their initial enthusiasm for celebrating entrance architecture is the reason why this book is before you. As well, coordinating editor Melina Deliyannis provided extremely valuable day-to-day guidance to ensure quality throughout the production process. All three made it a lot of fun.

There were many architects and interns at Hutton Ford Architects who contributed to the realization of these projects. In addition to the firm's two principals, associate Kari-elin Mock played a key role in many of the projects illustrated in this book. Our firm is run in an interactive studio format where design authorship is often the result of this collaborative process. We recognize the design contribution of the many talented current and past employees of Hutton Ford Architects.

We would also like to acknowledge the significant contribution of all the consultants and contractors who worked on these projects. Quality architecture does not happen without commitment at all levels.

Jennifer Seward's skill at using words to interpret and explain our architecture is fundamental to communicating our message. We are thankful for her diligence in finding the words to match the images. The contributions of Charles Romero and Chris Vandall in collating the project materials and the additional sketches by Mark Broyles, Heather Bock, and Kari-elin Mock were also critical and greatly appreciated.

Finally, we would like to thank our clients, teachers, and students who have informed and made these projects possible.

Alan Ford and Paul Hutton